8
WISE
WAYS
TO A HEALTHIER
HAPPIER MIND

8

WISE WAYS

TO A HEALTHIER
HAPPIER MIND

Kim Rutherford

London

The book information is catalogued as follows;
Author Name(s): Kim Rutherford
Title: 8 Wise Ways to a Healthier Happier Mind
Description; First Edition

1st Edition, 2021

Book Design by Leah Kent

ISBN (hardcover) 978-1-913479-93-0
ISBN (paperback) 978-1-913479-91-6
ISBN (ebook) 978-1-913479-92-3

Published by That Guy's House
www.ThatGuysHouse.com

To my husband and best friend, whose ongoing belief in me when I had none of my own has led to this book. You truly are what makes my life rich in every way, and I apologise for the days I forget that.

To Dr Miguel Montenegro, my mentor and friend, thank you for encouraging me to push forward and bring 8Wise™ to life in both my private practice and in this book.

To my clients, thank you for trusting me with your unique journey. I am forever changed by each one of you and in awe of your strength, your honesty and your overwhelming courage – it is you that makes me a better person and a better therapist.

In memory of those who are no longer with us, who enriched my life simply through being a part of it, no matter how briefly, your light still shines on, and it shines bright.

Finally, to you the reader, I hope that this book helps you find your unique path to a happier, healthier and fulfilling life – like it has for so many others. Always remember you are so much more than your darkest thoughts tell you. You have more strength and courage than you can ever imagine and on the dark days, of which we all experience, never feel alone, because if you reach out someone will always reach back; you just need to reach in the right direction. Because kindness can come from the strangest of places, so don't lose faith in the human race and never lose faith in yourself.

CONTENTS

Foreword

By Dr Miguel Montenegro

Clinical Psychologist

Statistics are quite attractive to make strong points and for that reason are often used in presentations and literature. As such, I am tempted to start using that tactic, perhaps to keep to the tradition but to also keep aligned to the message of this wonderful book – 'One in four people will experience a mental health problem of some kind each year in England' (according to Mind, 2020). Often, the 'one in four' come to seek treatment during crisis, and most often after years of enduring psychological distress.

I met Kim exactly three years ago in that context, both as professionals trained to treat the one in four people that come to our services. It was a chance encounter that would change my life forever, as I saw Kim's passions for her work and her 8Wise™ model being created, like a canvas painting develops right in front of our eyes. I was in awe from day one; her personality, wit, and knowledge reminded me why I had chosen to work in the field of mental health many years prior.

I must say I felt humbled when Kim asked me to read the first drafts of this book, and then join it with this foreword. It was such an honoured request, which I must confess left me a bit nervous about wanting to write something to the standard of this book. Reading this book made me think of a sonnet written in 1805 by my great-great-great-great-great-grandmother Catarina[1]. This poem, called 'Wondering thoughts', describes human experience with internal struggles with thoughts, beliefs and feelings, and how we can seek into ones' resources to achieve anchoring and wellness.

Looking out over the immense seas,
Then noticing the nearby white sand,
My thoughts and ideas are never bland,
Images of sorrow flow back with the breeze.

If I look up to put my thoughts at ease
I notice a battle in my mind's land,
And when these beliefs I try to command
Thousand evil thoughts bring me to my knees.

Subdued, invited by silence,
I give access to deep reflection,
Since I cannot fight with such defiance.

Suddenly I seek reason's protection
And shake away this internal violence,
I'm not that unhappy, despite my imperfection.

---

[1] Catarina de Lancastre (1749-1824)

As a clinical psychologist and psychotherapist, I am trained to deal with different levels of distress, but often people come to me exactly when they are in … distress, not before. Most models of therapy are exactly for that, to help people overcome distress after having experienced it, and not to prevent it. I have always been a great believer in prevention. There is a saying that I have always used as compass for my life, 'Prevention is better than cure,' and with that in mind I made my life journey to align my work and skills to ensure that people I work with understand the power of prevention. So, if we have treatment for the one in four, what do we have for the other three?

This book is meeting a need, the reach for the other three, but at the same time helping the one in four who has already experienced a mental health difficulty. Here we can find a manual and a workbook that reconnects the eight areas of wellness in a wise format, relevant for modern life, accessible for people who are very busy and often find they have little time to spend on themselves. I find it a refreshing approach to prevention, with an amazing focus on life as it happens, and an assurance that we are not just made of a psychological dimension, but also of a physical, spiritual, financial, social, and so on. Let's be wise and try the 8Wise™ model found in this book.

Introduction

A few years ago I was in a career I loved; I was a senior manager, travelling all across the UK meeting and educating amazing people who did amazing work. I was getting married, I was buying my first house, I had relocated to a stunning part of England – life on paper was good – but that all changed after a car crash that then led me into a spiral of emotional exhaustion and burnout, health anxiety, depression and even agoraphobia – not a fun experience.

I did all the right things; I put myself on a waiting list for a therapist and received my initial six sessions which brought a lot to the surface for me to then have to work through alone after the six sessions ended. I started to drown in my own emotions, my own thoughts and my own depression. I knew I needed to fight harder for myself, my life and my mental health, so I started working with an amazing private therapist who reintroduced me to myself.

What I learnt was that I am inquisitive, a problem solver, in need of clarity and process and I decided to use this to help myself. Whilst undergoing my own therapeutic journey, I was introduced to the concept of wellness a lot, and to be honest with you, I didn't have a clue what it was all about, and at the time I wasn't sure I even wanted to. I can honestly say I was ignorant to what wellness really was; I thought it was a buzz word for hippies, or personal trainers and nutritionists, after all, that is what the wellness market was selling me. My therapist would say to me at the end of each session, 'What are you going to do over the next week for your wellness?' and after a few weeks of blank faces and saying I would eat better (just to say something), I decided to get smart, get educated and help my own recovery process through implementing a wellness approach.

As I said, I am inquisitive, I am a problem solver, and I need clarity and confidence in something if I am going to commit to it. So, with wellness I researched, researched and researched some more until I got what I was looking for, something that connected to my experience, my goals as well as my personality (never underestimate the importance of your personality). Through my research, I learnt a lot about wellness and wellbeing, but nothing seemed to resonate with me until I came across the eight dimensions. Through learning and understanding more about them, I developed that focus on wellness actions that my therapist kept asking me to focus on. It was my new passion, my motivation, my purpose. It helped me crawl out of the depressive, dark, downward spiral I was in. It got me off of my butt fighting for a new life, one which led me to re-train in psychotherapy and develop my 8Wise™ Mental Wellness model that I want to share with you in this book.

My new career path helped me understand mental health differently, as a positive thing, as a superpower that we all have that can be channelled for effective wellness, and the eight dimensions provide the language and focus for that. But from my own experience I knew that for optimal benefit I needed to create a wellness formula that anyone could use, whether in or out of therapy, or whether they be in recovery from mental health issues or trying to protect their mental health in general. It was important to me to create something that could support all people with their mental health journey no matter at what stage they may be, and I wanted to give people their power back, to become the driving force behind their mental health rather than just sat in a reactive seat.

Now, I am not a numbers person, in fact, I don't enjoy maths at all, but I understand its success in problem solving through formulas and equations, and so I wanted to create a non-mathematical variation of that for wellness – and that is what 8Wise is.

I want to clarify from the offset that I did not create the eight dimensions of wellness – I came across them when researching therapeutic treatments and processes and found that the Substance Abuse and Mental Health Services Administration (SAMHSA) were using them as a way to focus on and optimise health for patients, and I think they saved my life.

Just like numbers are the language of math, for me the eight dimensions are the language of wellness, and my 8Wise model is a self-help mathematical equation. It is the problem-solving formula that puts you back in control of your wellness, enabling you to manage it effectively to support you in the longer-term protection of your mental and physical health (they go hand in hand).

This is a self-help book that can be used to protect your mental health, prevent mental health issues, or support with recovery. But to be clear about my self-help philosophy – there is no point in reading a 'self-help book' if you are unable to use the content or you are not going to do anything with the content. There is no point in investing in just the self-help book – you should be doing it to invest in your life. There is simply no point buying a book that could make your life better if it's just going to sit on a shelf gathering dust whilst your wellness suffers. So I want you to use this book to gain a deeper understanding of wellness and my 8Wise model, but more importantly I want you to use this book and develop your own effective lifelong strategies for wellness in order to protect your mental health – because prevention is always better than cure.

Whilst working your way through this book I recommend investing in either a notebook or the 8Wise Journal. The book is split into three core sections:

Part 1: Introduction to mental health and wellness

- Develop your knowledge on wellness and mental health triggers, signs and symptoms

Part 2: Introduction to the 8Wise model

- Develop your knowledge on the full spectrum of wellness and the 8Wise journey

Part 3: Taking Action

- Learn to use the 8Wise support tools

- Assess your wellness levels against the 8Wise framework

- Identify the main life events, traumas and transitions that are impacting your wellness

- Identify the biggest challenges linked to those life events, traumas and transitions

- Implement an effective transition plan for problem solving the challenges and moving forward towards improved health and wellbeing.

When I was a child, you could read books where you chose where the story led. At the end of a chapter you could choose between two different options and then move to the page that your chosen option was on. It always made me feel I had more control of the story and I liked that approach, so I have tried to provide an element of that in this book too. As I am sharing with you a tool to help you take back control of your mental health, I may as well start with giving you control of how you use that tool.

I recommend you read Chapters 1 to 6 in sequence, but after that you have two options:

- Option 1: Continue to read each chapter in sequence

- Option 2: Follow the prompts that enable you to move between specific sections of Part 2 and Part 3 out of sequence.

Both options will lead to the same outcome.

But what is this outcome?

By the end of this book, if you follow the directions, you will:

- have a clearer idea of your mental health, your triggers and your path for moving forward positively

- have completed self-evaluations of your current wellness levels and mental health risks

- have completed tasks to create a solid wellness foundation so you can develop an effective 8Wise Transition plan consisting of milestones and steps that help you to accomplish your goal of 'improving your wellness to protect your longer term mental and physical health'

- have life-long tools and techniques to help with your longer-term health and wellness plans.

I am sure the process will impact your life as positively as it has impacted my own, but as a practising psychotherapist it has also proven to be a beneficial approach for the clients that have experienced it over the past three years. Welcome to your 8Wise journey and enjoy learning your 8Wise steps to a healthier and happier mind.

PART ONE

Traumas, Triggers, and The Meaning of Life

Chapter 1:

The Other Three

I remember sitting in a musty smelling training room with dirty yellow walls, watching my colleague deliver mental health training to new mental health nurses. They were so passionate and keen to be their best in order to help others become their best; it was truly inspiring to see, which is why I opted to participate on this training as often as I could. I had seen this training so many times before and could practically recite it almost word for word, but on this day I remember one slide more than any others.

I remember the slide that changed my life: it flipped the switch in my brain as it vividly flashed on the bright glowing screen in all of its purple and pink glory – *'One in four people will experience a mental health problem of some kind each year in England,'* a statistic that is still confirmed by the charity Mind as a I write this book.

The figure comes from a study carried out on behalf of the NHS that sought to establish the mental health issues in people over the age of sixteen in the UK. The data is collated from a survey that focuses on those that confirmed they had felt symptoms within the past week. To clarify, these statistics are not set in stone; they are fluid, sometimes one in six, sometimes one in five, but one in four is the average.

It is a common statistic used within mental health training and literature, and one I had seen many times before, but it was at that moment I accepted, 'I am one of the one in four – but what I would do to be one of the "other three" again,' and without meaning to sound like a cliché – that's when it hit me. There are always two sides to a statistic; we just tend to focus on the one that is presented to us, and in this case, most of us ignore the 'other three' because we are so focused on the 'one in four'.

I was once one of the 'other three', but I developed into a 'one in four' when I started to experience emotional exhaustion and burnout which then led to anxiety, specifically health anxiety, that then developed into depression with agoraphobia thrown into the mix. If you are reading this and are currently experiencing mental health problems, you, like me, have been one of the 'other three' too, and if you are reading this and have never experienced a mental health problem or have fully recovered from a mental health issue then you are one of the 'other three'.

In that training room, my mind started to swirl, and my overthinking tendencies went into overdrive with question after question as I processed it all:

What could I have done to remain one of the 'other three'?

Why had no one ever taught me how to stay part of the 'other three'?

Every single person in that room was learning to look after the 'one in four', which is fantastic and very much needed, but where are those who want to work with the 'other three'? Because those people struggle too, and they may just be on the verge of struggling too much. It was then for the first time that I knew what I wanted to do, because the person in that room who wanted to focus on the 'other three' was me.

I wanted to focus on preventing people from developing the mental health issues that moved them into the 'one in four' statistic, because talking from personal and professional experience, being part of that statistic sucks.

Dysfunctional stress, burnout, anxiety and depression (my areas of specialism) are awful! I was miserable and each day was difficult, emotional and exhausting – it was like swimming through never-ending sludge in the dark and I wanted to protect as many people as possible from experiencing what I did, or at least reduce the amount of time they do. I still want that. People suffering bothers me and so many people are suffering. Realistically, I have always known I can't help everyone, but to be able to start helping as many as possible through focusing on the 'other three' has become my purpose, my focus, my mission.

But, back in that training room it was for personal reasons too that I wanted to get back to being part of the 'other three', because for some it is possible to recover. I was getting married to a wonderful man, we were starting our new life, we were genuinely blessed in so many ways (and still are). I didn't want to lose that, I didn't want to lose us and I sure as hell didn't want to lose me. As a child, I had seen first-hand how someone's mental health issues can steal years of their life, taking with it any chance of joy, happiness and the ability to create positive memories and experiences, not just for themselves but for their loved ones too. I didn't want that for myself or my family and friends, so I looked for inspiration, and it came from the other memory I had from my childhood, the one where I had seen someone fight their way out of that darkness. I knew then and still know to this day that it is possible to swim right through that sludge and out the other side, and so I created my 8Wise model to help you do exactly that. If you want to learn how to swim through the sludge, or stay out of it altogether, then my 8Wise model will guide you through it, leading you to improving your wellness and wellbeing so you can protect your longer-term mental and physical health, because prevention is better than cure. If you are going to be a mental health statistic, be one of the 'other three' rather than the 'one in four'.

Mental Health

We can't possibly talk about wellness and wellbeing without talking about mental health, and we can't talk about mental health unless we face the reality of what some people are calling a mental health crisis, due to the increasing mental health numbers year after year for over twenty years.

So, let's start with some clarification, because what will become a recurring theme throughout this book is that there is a lot of confusion about terminology, especially when it comes to mental health and mental illness. Personally, I was confused for a long time too, and I grew up with someone experiencing mental health issues as well experiencing the magic of my own. There is no shame in being confused.

What I have experienced, as you may have too, is that mental health and mental illness are often used interchangeably, which causes confusion, which then triggers a chain reaction in society. Confusion generates fear, fear generates stigma, stigma generates shame, and shame can lead to isolation, loneliness and suffering in silence. So, in my mind the first step to counteracting such a negative chain reaction in society is to provide clarity and clear up the confusion, starting with one simple question:

What is Mental Health?

Mental health refers to our emotional, psychological and social wellbeing. Everyone has mental health; it affects how we think, how we feel and how we behave. Being mentally healthy is just like being physically healthy, as it leads us to living a productive and fulfilling life. Over the years, I have always thought that if you pay for a gym membership to keep physically fit, then it would make sense to see a therapist to keep you mentally fit too. Good mental health means we are resilient and can handle life's challenges and stresses. It also means we can have meaningful relationships and make sound decisions for ourselves when it comes to life transitions or simply having to adapt or make changes.

Mental health is also understood as emotional health or wellbeing, and I will cover this more in later chapters. But the most common misinterpretation is that having mental health means having a mental health problem or mental illness, when really all it means is that you are coping with your life well, that you are engaged with friends, family and work, and you are emotionally balanced with effective thinking and decision-making skills that do not affect how you behave in a negative or dysfunctional way. Overall, to be mentally healthy means you are making the most of your life and your potential.

Just like with our physical health, sometimes we have up and down days. Sometimes you may get a cold which affects your physical health *(I am currently writing this with a toothache and head cold)*, and sometimes you might feel a little low in mood or anxious, which affects your mental health. Both scenarios tend to happen when we feel more stressed, run down, tired or have increased fears. But just like how the symptoms of the common cold may affect our physical health temporarily, they soon pass, and we start feeling better again. The same is for our mental health symptoms too; most of the time, they will simply pass by.

I am sure you have all experienced a bad day when you feel sad, or unhappy, a little fearful of things or experience a setback in some way that soon passes. This is understood to be a '**mild** *mental health problem*.' You have a small number of symptoms that have a limited effect on your daily life – this is a part of being mentally healthy, and your ability to bounce back from these moments is mentally healthy. For some, you may find those feelings or experiences don't pass by quickly and they develop into either a '**moderate** *mental health problem*,' when you have more symptoms that can make your daily life much more difficult than usual, or a '**severe** *mental health* *problem',* when you have many symptoms that can make your daily life extremely difficult. It is possible to move between all three levels, experiencing each level at different times.

But again, just like our physical health can go up and down as we experience illness, so can our mental health, and it can happen to anyone – no one is immune from that possibility. However, whilst one person may bounce back from a setback, someone else may struggle. Just as you may only get a cold for twenty-four hours, but for your friend it may develop into something else.

Your mental health does not stay linear – it is not like calm, still waters; instead, it reacts to the life events and circumstances you and I experience, like waves. Just as your life moves through different stages, so will your mental health. It is important to be open and honest with yourself and others when you have those difficult days, because ignoring them or hiding them can exacerbate them, leading you to further mental health problems, which is why mental health stigma is such a dangerous thing. Stigma leads people to feeling uncomfortable about experiencing symptoms that may indicate mental health problems, and so they don't open up or talk about it. So, if there is one thing I want you to take away from this book, it is this ...

> It is normal to experience low mood, bad days, sad days and overwhelming feelings of stress, fear and exhaustion. You are not weak, you are not limited, you are not mentally unstable...

...you are simply human, and it is healthy to not only know and understand how you are feeling, but also to talk about it openly and honestly to ensure your long-term mental health. So don't feel shame and don't hide it – let someone know and get help if you think you need it, because ignoring it can lead to longer-term symptoms that are harder to manage. You want to protect your mental health just as much as you want to protect your physical health so you can live a long and happy life.

To summarise: *Mental health involves effectively functioning in our daily activities, resulting in healthy relationships, an ability to adapt, change and cope with adversity and participate productively in activities such as school, work and caregiving.*

I hope this has cleared up the meaning of mental health for you a little so we can explore the opposite side of the coin, which is mental illness.

What is Mental Illness?

Before I begin this section, I want to reiterate that this book is not to replace a formal diagnosis. A mental illness can only, and should only, be diagnosed by a mental health professional, so if you feel you are experiencing any of the symptoms outlined, please contact your doctor.

As a child, I watched a loved one going in and out of hospital as they battled their mental health problems, and therefore I thought that mental illness led you into hospital. As an adult who now understands mental illness, I know now it actually refers to a wide range of mental health problems, conditions and disorders that affect mood, thinking and behaviour.

Like heart disease, mental illness is perceived by many to also be a medical problem *(although this is currently a topic of hot debate after the work of Lucy Johnstone and Mary Bole was published in the 'Power Threat Meaning Framework' (PTMF)).*

Mental illnesses are health problems and conditions involving changes in emotion, thinking or behaviour that are linked with distress and/or problems functioning in life. You will sometimes hear the term 'mental health problems' used instead of 'mental illnesses', but they are the same thing.

If a **'mild** *mental health problem'* develops into ongoing signs and symptoms that cause you frequent stress and affect your ability to function, it can lead to either a **'moderate** *mental health problem'* or a **'severe** *mental health problem',* depending on how the person is affected by their symptoms. *In my private practice, I work with mild to moderate mental health problems only and signpost those experiencing severe mental health problems to expert mental health clinicians. I do this because it is important for my clients to receive the best care available to them, and from my perspective that means having access to a wider set of specialisms and skills than just my own.*

There is no timeline attached to mental illness – it can be occasional or long-lasting, and there is no single cause either. Research indicates that there are a number of factors that can contribute to it, and it is helpful to know what these are.

1. Biological Factors

Our brain functions through chemicals called neurotransmitters communicating to different parts of the brain through pathways. Common belief within clinical psychology is that when we have an abnormal function within these pathways, it can become a factor that can lead to mental illness. Psychotherapy and medication can help those pathways to run more efficiently. There have been recent studies that counter this argument (Lucy Johnstone, 'Good Practice Guidelines on the Use of Psychological Formulation' – Division of Clinical Psychology, 2011) but it still remains the dominant diagnosis process for clinical psychologists and psychiatrists.

Other biological factors that may also aid the development of a mental illness are family history, infections, brain damage through injury, brain defects, prenatal damage, substance abuse and poor nutrition.

2. Psychological Factors

If a child experiences a severe trauma, this can lead to psychological factors which may contribute to developing mental health illness. Traumatic experiences could include the loss of a parent, neglect or abuse (emotional, physical or sexual).

3. Environmental Factors

Within the world of clinical psychology, environmental factors are the most important factors, because issues such as trauma, socialisation and poverty are often the precipitators of mental illness. This is because if a person is susceptible to mental illness due to any of the causes outlined previously, then additional stressors can trigger their mental health issues. Stressors include a dysfunctional family, low self-esteem, anxiety, transitional periods like changing jobs or schools, relocating, moving house, death or divorce, social or cultural expectations, and direct or indirect substance abuse.

A combination of these factors can lead to a wide range of mental illness, including but not limited to:

Anxiety

Anxiety is a feeling of fear, dread, and uneasiness about something going wrong in the future. We can all feel anxiety from time to time, but it develops into a disorder when the anxiety does not reduce or pass, and instead it increases and continues, which affects you physically, emotionally and socially. Anxiety disorders include generalised anxiety disorder (GAD), panic disorder and phobias.

Bipolar

Formerly known as manic depression, bipolar is a mood disorder where the person feels extreme high moods, known as manic or hypomanic episodes, or extreme low depressive moods and can potentially have some psychotic symptoms during either episode. Due to the extreme mood swings, for someone diagnosed with bipolar it can be difficult to manage everyday tasks or maintain relationships, and although there is no cure for bipolar, there are many treatment options that can help manage the symptoms.

Depression

Depression is a mood disorder and people who suffer from it may experience strong feelings of sadness, helplessness or a lack of interest in activities they once enjoyed. It can interfere with your day-to-day life, affect your relationships and even lead to physical health issues such as headaches or chronic body pain. Depression symptoms can range from mild to severe, and typically include low mood, weight loss or gain, insomnia or sleeping too much, fatigue, feelings of worthlessness or guilt, lack of concentration and thoughts about death or suicide.

Obsessive-Compulsive Disorder (OCD)

Many people suffer from Obsessive-Compulsive Disorder (OCD). People who have OCD experience obsessive thoughts and compulsive behaviours. It is a form of anxiety disorder which is characterised by uncontrollable, unwanted thoughts and ritualised, repetitive behaviours that people who experience OCD feel compelled to perform. Those who suffer with OCD tend to obsess over an unwanted and unpleasant thought, image or urge that repeatedly enters their mind. Those who have OCD likely understand that their thoughts and behaviours are irrational but are still unable to resist them and break the habit.

Panic Disorder

In simple terms, this is a condition where the fear of having a panic attack itself leads the person to have a panic attack. Panic attacks are a sudden episode of extreme fear that trigger a range of intense mental and physical symptoms. Alongside the fear that triggers an initial panic attack, the attack itself is extremely frightening. For some people it can feel very similar to a heart attack, leaving someone feeling like they might be dying. High levels of stress can lead to panic attacks, but it is only diagnosed as a panic disorder if there is a constant fear of experiencing another attack.

PTSD

Post-traumatic stress disorder (PTSD) is a form of anxiety that is caused by experiencing extremely stressful, scary or distressing events. Those who suffer from the disorder tend to relive these experiences through nightmares or flashbacks and sometimes have uncontrollable thoughts about the event. They may feel isolated, irritated and even guilty. PTSD can also cause insomnia and make it difficult to concentrate, meaning it can have a huge effect on someone's daily life.

There are more than 200 classified forms of mental illness, with each having its own symptoms, so there is no standard set of common symptoms for mental health illnesses, which is why stereotyping people with mental illness leads to ongoing stigma, misunderstanding and ignorance. The first thing to learn is that mental illness is never a one-size-fits-all condition

– it's much more complex than that. Hence, it needs to be diagnosed by a professional.

To summarise: *The term 'mental illness' collectively refers to all professionally diagnoseable* mental health illnesses, problems, disorders and conditions that involve distress and/or problems functioning in social, work or family activities. It involves significant changes in a person's thinking, emotions and behaviours.*

* Diagnoseable by a medical or mental health professional, therefore if you believe you are experiencing any of the symptoms outlined in this book please visit your doctor or a mental health practitioner.

What Does the Data Tell Us?

Now that we have more clarity regarding what mental health is, what mental illness is, and how they might be affecting us, it leads us back to ask the question: Is there really a mental health crisis happening? I get asked this question a lot by podcasters, bloggers, clients, friends, peers and family. And for us to answer it, we have to look to the statistics for some guidance and insight.

Before I provide any data, I want to warn you that because a lot of the data relies heavily on people self-reporting how they feel, it can never be 100% accurate. We also need to take into consideration many people never get diagnosed as they never seek treatment. But of all the data that exists, some of the most reliable is that produced by the Institute of Health Metrics

(IHME) which showed a global figure of 792 million people in 2017 suffering with some kind of mental illness, which is 10.7% of the world's population or 13% if you include drugs and alcohol issues too.

On a global scale, 300 million people suffered from anxiety, 160 million from major depressive disorder and another 100 million from mild depression. Further statistics showed high levels of bipolar, eating disorders (anorexia and bulimia) and schizophrenia. The table below outlines this further.

Disorder	Share of population with disorder	Number of people with the disorder	Males : Females with disorder
Any mental disorder	10.7%	792 million	9.3% M 11.9% F
Depression	3.4%	264 million	2.7% M 4.1% F
Anxiety disorders	3.8%	284 million	2.8% M 4.7%F
Bipolar disorder	.9%	46 million	0.55% M 0.65% F
Eating disorders	0.2%	16 million	0.13% M 0.29% F
Schizophrenia	0.3%	20 million	0.26% M 0.25% F
Any mental or substance use disorder	13%	970 million	12.6% M 13.3% F
Alcohol use disorder	1.4%	107 million	2% M 0.8% F
Drug use disorder (excluding alcohol)	0.9%	71 million	1.3% M 2.6% F

Findings from the Global Burden of Disease Study 2017

I personally was not surprised to find that richer nations dominate the list of countries most burdened by the full range of mental illnesses, and that approximately eight million people die each year due to mental illness. Rich nations create a lot of external triggers that influence and effect our internal triggers – something I will touch upon in later chapters.

As a Brit, I always look to my 'home' statistics first as it's important to know what's happening on your own doorstep and what might be happening to your neighbour. The British charity Mind refers to the statistic that triggered my passion of working with the 'other three' I have previously talked about. Mind provides some truly thought-provoking statistics:

- At any given time, one in six working-age adults have symptoms associated with mental ill health

- Mental illness is the second-largest source of burden of disease in England. Mental illnesses are more common, long-lasting and impactful than other health conditions

- People with a long-term mental health condition lose their jobs every year at around double the rate of those without a mental health condition. This equates to 300,000 people – the equivalent of the population of a small city

- 75% of mental illness starts before age eighteen

- Men aged 40-49 have the highest suicide rates in the UK

- 70-75% of people with diagnosable mental illness receive no treatment at all

- The amount of people with common mental health problems went up by 20% between 1993 to 2014, in both men and women

- The percentage of people reporting severe mental health symptoms in any given week rose from 7% in 1993, to over 9% in 2014.

I am not going to tell you there is a global mental health crisis, or that the numbers are increasing dramatically year by year, even if it looks like they are; instead, I will leave you to draw your own conclusions. My belief is that there is now more awareness of mental health and specifically the symptoms of mental illness, and so more cases are now recorded. There is, however, an increase in mental health cases for young people and this will no doubt be impacting the overall statistics.

What I want to talk about is that one specific statistic that I mentioned at the start of the chapter: **one in four people will experience some form of mental illness in any given year.**

My questions regarding this are:

- If the one in four people who experience a mental health condition can access support and treatment, then what about the 'other three'?

- What are we doing to protect the 'other three' from developing a mental illness? What are we doing to prevent the 'other three' from developing into one of those statistics?

- Can mental illness ever really be prevented?

- What are you doing to protect your longer-term mental health?

I first want to clarify something with you, which is that there is no definitive way to prevent mental illness – just like there is no definitive way to cure it. However, there is evidence that if you have a mental illness, you can help manage and reduce your symptoms by taking steps to control any stress, increase your resilience and boost low self-esteem. Now, here is the big question – if these things can help alleviate symptoms, is it also possible that they can offer some protection from developing these symptoms too?

Prevention

Preventing the onset of mental health problems before they occur is an important approach to protecting both our long term mental and physical health. As I have said before, mental health prevention has been my core focus for a long time now, through my own mental health journey and through the research I completed to support myself and then my own clients. But it is also important for you to understand that the 8Wise model that I will be walking you through in later chapters can be used as both a prevention model and a recovery model. It can help to prevent the 'other three' from becoming part of the mental illness statistics. It can also be used to support those who are experiencing mild or moderate mental health problems too, by leading them back to becoming part of the 'other three' again and protecting their overall wellness and wellbeing. Someone with severe mental health problems can also benefit from the 8Wise approach as part of an overarching clinical plan, providing it is agreed to by a mental health clinician. It is, however, by no means a replacement for any medication or recovery plan prescribed by a clinical mental health practitioner.

With mental health statistics so high on a global scale, it is not surprising that some global leaders have been looking at ways to change this. Prevention strategies have become part of global mental health agenda and fall into three core preventative approaches:

Primary Prevention

This approach aims to stop mental health problems before they occur through educating communities to improve their wellness and wellbeing and by reducing stigma through empathy, understanding and education.

Secondary Prevention

This approach aims to support those at a higher risk of developing mental health problems caused by biological factors such as genetics, dysfunctions within the brain and brain injuries. It can also support those who are at risk due to life experiences and exposure to childhood traumas.

Tertiary Prevention

This approach aims to support those living with mental health problems by reducing symptoms and empowering people to manage their own symptoms as much as possible to improve their wellness and wellbeing so they can have a better quality of life.

From this, we can see that there is some thought being put into the 'other three' by global leaders, which is positive. But still the mental health approach remains predominantly reactive, focusing on medication and treatment to treat the problem, rather than proactive, using tools to prevent the problem from occurring in the first place. A proactive approach could utilise wellness and wellbeing programmes that are not just centred around mindfulness, exercise and nutrition (though these are all extremely important) but also look at the person holistically. By widening the wellness spectrum from just physical and emotional, and by incorporating self-reflection, problem solving and self-acceptance, we can be empowered to manage our own mental health proactively, which will have a positive effect on our physical health too – leading to a happier and healthier life.

This concept has been my driver; I wanted to create a model that any person, at any time could access. I wanted to create something for 'the other three' as well as the one in four. I wanted to create something that you don't need to go on a waiting list for and that you don't have to get prescribed onto or wait for a formal diagnosis to access it. I wanted to create something that wasn't limited or restricted by time constraints, funding or personal finances.

I felt there was a need to provide an approach that puts you back in control of your mental health, that allows you to learn about yourself, that gives you the guidance to develop in the areas that support you to take action to improve your wellness and wellbeing for a longer, happier and more fulfilling life.

It was important to me to have a collaborative model that works alongside all the other treatments and health professionals who provide amazing health and happiness services so who ever accesses it can truly create their own personalised wellness and wellbeing tool belt for living a happier and healthier life.

But most of all, I don't want to just smash the stigma of mental health – I want to make mental health something positive we think about, something positive we talk about, something that empowers us to truly live a happy and healthy life for as long as we can, for our friends, for our loved ones and most importantly, for ourselves.

I truly believe that we should all aim to improve our wellness, to protect our mental and physical health, because prevention is better than cure, and that is what the 8Wise model is all about.

Chapter 2:

The Meaning of Life

Let's get philosophical for a moment. What I love about the philosophical and scientific debates is they both lead to each other. From a philosophical question comes a scientific theory, and from a scientific theory we get new philosophical questions, and so I want to start with the biggest philosophical question of them all – What is the meaning of life?

Growing up, I was a really shy child, short, dumpy and an introverted observer (not a lot has changed other than that I am no longer shy). In truth, people scared me, and so books were my best friends, and this led to me also being a very annoying child because those books led me to become the 'why' child. I wanted to know the 'why' behind everything. I was a pain in the butt with the constant questioning, and one of my ongoing questions was 'Why are we here?', which led to me asking 'What is the meaning of life?' I would ask my parents, my teachers, my Sunday school teachers, my friends, my friends' parents, the librarian – I would ask anyone I felt comfortable talking to. In fact, from as young as I can remember, I have always been more interested in discussions, debate and deep thoughts about the 'big' questions than any of the fun and frolics most young people are into. Don't get me wrong, I am not a saint, I have had my fair share of 'fun and frolics' and dancing on tables. But I always preferred to be sat reading or in deep discussion about a topic I was passionate about … and to be fair, I still am.

I welcome discussion about this topic, and I am not alone, because this is the question that people have been trying to answer since the dawn of time. We are always searching for greater meaning to somehow prove to ourselves, to our species, that there is more to our experience in this world, in our short life. We need to know that there is a plan or a purpose – otherwise what's the point to it all?!

Do you yourself ask the big questions? Do you want to know, like I do:

- What's the point to the madness in our lives and in the world?

- Is there a point to all the chaos?

- Do the traumas and upset we experience have a meaning?

- What's the point of being good, bad, healthy, unhealthy, spiritual, unspiritual?

- What's the point in making the most of our mortality?

- What's the point in respecting the air in our lungs and the life in our beings?

- What is the point of anything?

But why does it matter though? Why do we as a human race need answers to why we exist? Why can we not be satisfied that we simply do and leave it at that? Why do we need answers?

In my years of discussing this topic, I have learnt that some people need answers as certainty brings comfort in the dark times. Such as when we lose a loved one, when we get terminally ill, when we experience a great tragedy or when we see such obscene suffering across the planet – we need for it to make sense. In those moments, comfort may make it all a little more bearable.

For some, the questions and answers bring understanding, and that understanding creates drive, a motivation and a purpose to live a life where legacy of worth exists after we are gone – that way, through our legacy, we can live forever and there is no ending.

For others, the search for answers comes from ego and arrogance, the unwillingness to acknowledge or accept that maybe this is it, maybe we simply are not the most important beings in the universe – maybe there is no point to us as a human race and therefore, no importance to us as a living person. Maybe we are just pointless.

Then of course there are those who don't ask at all – maybe they don't want to know, maybe they don't need to know, maybe for them simply existing is more important than thinking about the possible why we exist.

I don't think there is any such thing as a right need or a wrong need – you have yours, they have theirs and I have mine. My need for answers comes from wanting to have full control over my life – a recurring theme that has always brought me many more problems and questions than it has ever brought solutions and answers. I came to this realisation the hard way, and although my need for control has reduced dramatically (my sister definitely disagrees with this), I still remain inquisitive, I still want answers, I still feel the need to understand.

Through my ongoing questioning, discussion and debates regarding the meaning of life, I have drawn my own conclusions and so personally I think there is a point to life. In fact, I think there is more than one point to the meaning of life and human existence. I think we get confused between the concept of 'the meaning of life' and living 'a meaningful life', and the two are very different – but both are extremely valid points.

A Meaningful Life

In positive psychology, a meaningful life is the concept of having purpose, significance, fulfilment, and satisfaction of life. It is an internal focus, an independent focus, even a selfish focus. It is the belief that our own personal life is meaningful and that there is somehow a connection between the external world and the internal world we exist in – the physical world and the spiritual world. As if what we do, feel and think has an impact on the world around us, whether that be with regard to the energy it creates or affects in this life or, as some belief systems state, how it impacts in the afterlife and in the next life. In positive psychology, it is believed that those who possess such a sense of meaning are generally happier than those who do not. They experience lower levels of negative emotions and therefore are less at risk of mental illness compared to those who have yet to find meaning in their life and therefore experience more increased levels of negative emotions and thoughts. So, it could be argued that the main purpose for identifying or understanding what it is to live 'a meaningful life' is for our mental wellness, our longer-term mental health, our overall wellness and wellbeing. Therefore, to live a meaningful life could simply mean to stay well. Thomas Kitwood claimed, in his model of psychological needs, that to feel well and to feel balanced we needed love, comfort, identify, occupation, inclusion and attachment, and with those elements we can successfully live a meaningful life.

The Meaning of Life

Now, the meaning of life takes us to a whole new level. The crux of the question is simply, 'What is the significance of humans living or existing at all?' Therefore, for me, the question really means 'What is the meaning of human life?' or 'What is the point in our species?' The search for the answer to this question has kept philosophers, scientists, theologists and metaphysicists busy for millennia. Different people and different cultures believe different things, and so no final answer has ever been agreed upon. Therefore, as a species we continue to search for our meaning, our purpose, trying to seek a connection between our existence and something more tangible. The religious argument focuses on symbolic meaning: the soul, good and evil, created by the divine and, of course, the importance of love and free will. The scientific argument focuses more on empirical belief, the connection between the power of our senses, the biological and chemical makeup of our physical being, and the energy of the immediate environment and the wider universe.

I went to Sunday school and church as a child, but I am not religious, and I would not label myself a scientist or a philosopher either. I like to think of myself as balanced somewhere between all three. But along with those who do align themselves to those categories, I have contemplated these two questions myself:

- What is the meaning of life?

- What is it to have meaning in life?

I have developed my own theory, my own philosophy, my own belief based on the information provided by those that have researched and debated the questions before me.

My Meaning of Life

Now to make it clear, this is 'MY' meaning of life, not 'THE' meaning of life – it is how I perceive and interpret the world and the information provided about it. It is my philosophy and my belief. If you agree with it, then great; if you disagree with it, then that's great too, and I would be interested in hearing your philosophy on the topic someday. But as we are focusing on 'my meaning of life', I am going to first start to look at 'What does "life" mean?'

The dictionary defines 'life' as:

1. The condition that distinguishes animals and plants from inorganic matter, including the capacity for growth, reproduction, functional activity, and continual change preceding death. This can be seen as the 'origins of life';

2. The existence of an individual human being or animal.

My simple interpretation of this is that we exist and so we have life, we die and so we have life, and we function, so we have life, and it this understanding that I base my ideas on.

So, let's start with question one: 'What is the meaning of life?'

My answer to this question comes in two parts:

- Part one: Survival

- Part two: Evolution

Part One: Survival

I believe that 'survival' is one element of 'the meaning of life' because we have an inbuilt system that specifically caters for it. If we have an inbuilt system for it, then to me that indicates it is pretty important to humans to stay alive and to survive. In fact, you could argue that it lies at the heart of everything we do. It is our driving force – our ultimate purpose is to stay alive, to keep living, to extend our mortality. Our inbuilt survival system allows us to know we are in danger, pre-warning us so we can react effectively and remove ourselves from that danger. Danger could be anything that our mind perceives as a threat to our life, to *the capacity for growth, reproduction, functional activity, continual change and existence*, as outlined by the definition of 'life'.

Our inbuilt survival system has the ability to affect the way our body functions and how our brain and mind works. I often argue that this system is our superhero response system. Instead of having to rush into a telephone booth to change when we sense danger, like Superman does, our survival system flips its switch on inside our brain, and, almost instantaneously, we become supercharged versions of ourselves. Now, that is pretty spectacular, but how does the survival system actually work?

Our survival system is commonly known as the 'fight or flight response'. Our brain and bodies are hardwired to not only identify dangers but also to adapt in order to survive those dangers. We have a structure in our brain that manages all of this, which I like to think of as our survival control tower; it's also known as the limbic system.

The limbic system is a group of interconnected structures located deep within the brain, and it's the part of the brain that's responsible for behavioural and emotional responses – specifically the behaviours needed for survival, such as feeding, reproduction, caring for our young and the fight or flight responses.

Summary: *It is the control centre for managing our survival.*

Other structures, such as the thalamus and basal ganglia (reward processing, habit formation, movement and learning), are also involved in the actions of the limbic system, but the three major structures I want to focus on are the hippocampus, amygdala and the hypothalamus.

Hippocampus

The hippocampus plays a critical role in our ability to function, as it is the memory centre of our brains. It is also connected to our ability to learn and can be easily affected by neurological and psychiatric conditions. The hippocampus is like a giant library in our brain that manages the information of our memories, organises them and stores the new memories effectively. It also connects certain sensations and emotions to these memories, and so we are able to associate memories with various senses, such as specific food aromas with memories of home, festivities and celebrations.

Summary: *I worked in the corporate world, and so I imagine that this is our internal data base, storing our memories and connecting them to our senses like folders and files.*

Amygdala

The amygdala processes our emotions and feelings, such as pleasure, fear, anxiety and anger. Like the hippocampus, it is also able to make connections to memories and so plays an important role in determining how effectively, efficiently and robustly those memories are stored. The stronger the memory, the longer it sticks, and so the amygdala has the ability to modify the strength and emotional content of memories and can form new ones, specifically related to fear, which are both strong and highly emotionally charged and so stay with us for longer. Most emotions possess a specific tone (positive or negative) and an intensity (low to high) that reflects emotional arousal. The amygdala's role is to risk-manage the danger in relation to the intensity and emotional tone content of fear memories and set off the warning alarm.

Summary: In my mind, this is the risk manager for all of the external stimuli that triggers intense emotional responses related to fear memories.

Hypothalamus

The hypothalamus may only be small, but it has a very big job as it plays a crucial role in hormone production and helps to stimulate many important processes in the body, such as releasing hormones, regulating body temperature, maintaining physiological cycles, controlling appetite, managing of sexual behaviour and regulating emotional responses.

The hypothalamus activates the fight or flight response, our internal survival system, by sending signals through specific nerves to the adrenal glands that then pump adrenaline into the bloodstream. The adrenaline triggers physiological changes such as the heart beating faster, pushing blood to the muscles and other vital organs, increasing blood pressure, affecting breathing, which then increases alertness, making all the senses become sharper.

Glucose also triggers increasing energy levels – leaving you feeling energised, focused and pumped – like a superhero ready to battle whatever has triggered the fear.

The three structures work closely together to provide us with our survival system. If the corporate world analogy of a data base does not work for you then I also like to think of it as a cruise ship. Imagine you are a large cruise ship casually drifting along the journey of your life, with your focus being on the journey and not the destination. You have various adventures along the way and want the journey to continue for as long as possible and to be as tranquil as possible. To ensure that happens, you have some specific roles in place on your ship:

1. You have your control tower that manages the journey and the response systems of the ship (the limbic system);

2. You have the database that logs and catalogues every adventure (like the Captain's log on Star Trek) so that you can remember them and learn from them in order to maintain a tranquil yet exciting journey (the hippocampus);

3. You have the risk manager who keeps a look out on the open waters to make sure that the ship is never in any danger or that the journey doesn't end too soon (the amygdala);

4. You have the communications manager who sends messages to a wide range of functions across the ship to make sure it is prepared for any situation.

In the case of an emergency, the control tower receives information, and this information is moved to the database for storage. The risk manager assesses it to see if the information highlights a risk to the journey. If the risk manager assesses that it is indeed a risk, then it triggers the alarm to the communications manager who then informs a range of functions across the ship to prepare it for steering through the storm ahead. The ship's survival chances depend on how healthy and robust the ship is and the effectiveness of the functions it has in place for managing stormy weathers. You could say that the ship has all the inbuilt functions to survive, but if it is not maintained, if it doesn't adapt to the challenges, if it doesn't sometimes change direction for calmer waters then the wellness of the ship suffers, reducing its chances of survival.

Based on this, my belief is that one element of the meaning of life is '**survival**' because, as demonstrated, we have a spectacular system built for it that affects us greatly every day of our life. Isn't that amazing? Isn't your body amazing? Aren't you amazing?

But the amazing doesn't stop there, because I believe there are two elements to the meaning of life and the second is '**evolution**'.

Part Two: Evolution

Evolution is the gradual development of something. In biology, it is about how the genes change from one generation to the next, changing our characteristics, as outlined through Darwin's evolution of humans, 'from primate to man' in its most simple terms. But, in my theory, evolution links more to knowledge and learning, how information is shared from one generation to the next, changing our mindset, our understanding and therefore helping us to grow and survive as both an individual and also as a species in the ever-changing world in which we exist.

Survival focuses on the individual, but how does that benefit the human race as a species? How can that alone be the 'meaning of life'? In my opinion, it can't be, and so my theory is that each person plays a role within the human race – you play a vital role within the survival and continuation of the human race – that's how amazing you are.

You see, my theory of the meaning of life has been developed alongside my growing knowledge, experience and fascination with personality types. 'Personality types' refers to the psychological classification of different types of individuals which, as a theory, dates back as far as the ancient Greece with Hippocrates (370 - 460 BC), but was later developed further by Carl Jung in 1921 in his book *Personality Types*.

I think having an understanding of personality types gives us better insight into who we are, as well as how and why we make the decisions that we do in our lives. Through understanding ourselves, we can then start to develop a better understanding towards the decisions of others, which I believe can lead to more empathy between us all.

So to get your personality type juices flowing, the core concept is that there are four functions, that then break into two pairs of cognitive functions.

Cognitive functions	Four Functions	
Irrational (perceiving) functions: sensation and intuition, which help us gather information	Sensation	Gathering information through trusting what we perceive to be concrete evidence.
	Intuition	Trusting hypothetical and unconscious gut instinct.
Rational (judging) functions: thinking and feeling, which help us make judgements to make decisions	Thinking	Being personally detached from the decision-making process using only data and logic.
	Feeling	Making decisions based on personal worth, such as like or dislike.

Please note, these are unconscious process preferences, not abilities. It doesn't mean that someone who prefers the thinking process is better at making a decision than the person who prefers a feeling process. From a psychological perspective both are equally rational when it comes to making decisions. It is not about one function being better than the other; it is simply about one function using a different process than the other to come to the same outcome – which is making a decision.

Just as you have got your head around that bit, let me throw something else into the mix, because flowing throughout all four functions is one of two energies or attitudes known as extroversion or introversion.

Energy		What to look for
Extroversion	Outward-turning energy that supports the cognitive function to operate effectively in the external world of behaviour, action, people, and things	• Action-oriented • Seeks to influence using a wide variety of knowledge • Prefers frequent interaction and recharges batteries by spending time with people
Introversion	Inward-turning energy that supports the cognitive function to operate effectively in the internal world of ideas and reflection	• Thought-oriented • Seeks to influence using a depth of knowledge • Prefers a more substantial interaction and recharges batteries by spending time alone.

But introversion and extroversion are not black and white – it is not one or the other. There are a range of characteristics that sit on a sliding scale, and you have the ability to move up and down that scale, even though in general you may lean towards one end of it more than the other. Hence an extrovert may like to recharge their batteries alone from time to time, just like an introvert may want to recharge socially.

Have a think about what you might be. Have a think about what your nearest and dearest might be, and based on what I have told you about me, what do you think I might be? You can also complete a wide range of personality assessments to determine your personality type – all of my clients complete one when they work with me on my 8Wise programme.

But for now, back to my theory – when you put together the different combinations of function you get a personality type:

- **Analysts**: Intuitive and thinking personality types, known for their rationality, impartiality and intellectual excellence

- **Diplomats**: Intuitive and feeling personality types, known for their empathy, sensitive skills and passionate idealism

- **Sentinels**: Observant and judging personality types, known for their practicality and focus on order, security and stability

- **Explorers**: Observant and prospecting personality types, known for their spontaneity, ingenuity and flexibility.

In theory, these personality types create roles within the human race, and this is how I think we use them.

To go back to our cruise ship analogy – we all head out on our cruise ships on the journey of our life, experiencing new adventures, learning to adapt in order to survive, gathering information, learning new things, discovering new findings and developing our knowledge, all based on the personality type we have or the role we have.

We share all of this information through books, social media, friends, family, work and education environments, so that others can use it to help themselves adapt and survive on their journey. Those who receive that information then do the same;

they gather skills, knowledge and information that then they then also pass down, so that each generation that comes after can explore and experience life for themselves but with more knowledge than those that came before them. They then feed back their findings and learnings to others and this process happens over and over again, evolving the human race with each cycle ensuring the continued survival of our species.

So, for the human race to survive, it needs to keep evolving, and to keep evolving, all humans need to survive as long as possible in order to gather relevant information and adapt and grow from that information. And guess what – we have an inbuilt system for that too – it's called 'learning' and our brains handle it very well.

So How Does Learning Happen?

We gather information through our senses: sight, hearing, taste, smell and touch. That information is transmitted through nerve cells called sensory neurons, by junctions between two nerve cells known as synapses along the neural pathway. They are then stored temporarily in short-term memory, which is the receiving centre for all sensory information we encounter day to day.

Once the information is processed in short-term memory, our brain's neural pathways carry the memories to the structural core, where they are compared with existing memories and stored in our long-term memory, with almost everything else we have ever experienced in our lives. Because this happens so quickly, by bouncing off so many different elements in the brain, some of the memory can get lost or cut off, which is why many of the memories we have are incomplete, and we fill them with what we think happened rather than what did happen.

This is the process that enables us to learn; we gather information and retain it in our short-term memory until it becomes strong enough for it to be moved into our long-term memory. Stronger memories are easier to recall, and memories become stronger through repeated exposure. This is why in learning we say, 'practice makes perfect' or 'repetition, repetition, repetition', as these processes help us to learn more, become better and develop stronger long-term memories.

When we recall a memory, we never actually recall the original memory; instead, it's a bit like watching a movie in that we can't experience the event exactly how it was, and instead the brain goes into rewind and replay mode. In your first experience of the event, you are the actor in the movie, but when recalling it as a memory, you are watching yourself act in the movie.

Memories that are strong and forged from experiences that had specific emotional tones and intensity (see Amygdala) stay with us a lifetime, and these tend to be the ones we share as learning for others to grow from.

And so, in answer to question one – 'What is the meaning of life?'– I believe it is to survive as individuals for as long as possible in order to gather as much information for the next generation to learn from so that we can evolve as a species.

In answer to question two – 'What is a meaningful life?' – I believe this is to live a life where you fulfil your 'role' in the evolution process. By this, I mean engage in amazing adventures and learn enough to pass on to others. To do this requires you to maintain optimum health and wellness, both mentally and physically. You need to build and maintain a strong ship in order for the journey of your life to be truly meaningful.

To summarise my philosophy with an analogy (and I do love an analogy): *The human race is a never-ending fleet of cruise ships, each built with an amazing system for surviving the high seas through any storm. Their mission is to go further than those who went before them and to teach those that come after to go further than they will ever go. And that is why the meaning of life for me is 'Survival' and 'Evolution'; to ensure the long-term survival of the human race, you as an individual play a fundamental part – that is how important you are.*

But what has all this got to do with mental health, wellness and wellbeing?

Well, your biological makeup, meaning the biological makeup of a human being, provides you with the potential answer to the ultimate philosophical question, 'What is the meaning of life?' You don't have to agree with mine – you have to decide for yourself if it is an important question to ask, and if it is, why.

For me, the importance of this question leads to other questions:

- Question 1: *What is the meaning of life?* which leads to…

- Question 2: *What is the meaning of my life?* which leads to…

- Question 3: *What is my purpose of life?* which leads to…

- Question 4: *Am I living a meaningful life?* which leads to…

- Question 5: *Am I living a happy and healthy life?* which leads to…

- Question 6: *Are **you** living a happy and healthy life?*

The 8Wise model that I will be sharing with you will not only help you to answer this final question; it will also help you achieve it with the support of philosophy, science and your own personal experiences and beliefs. It will help you get wise about your wellness so that you can live a meaningful life, because to live a meaningful life is to live a happy and healthy life, which is crucial for your survival, and I believe your survival is crucial for your core purpose, which is to help the human species evolve.

That's how important YOU are. That's how amazing YOU are. That's how awesome YOU are. Are you ready to believe that?

Chapter 3:

The Truth About Wellness and Wellbeing

What do you think of when you think of wellness and wellbeing? Do you think they are philosophical or are they scientific? There is sometimes confusion with regards to what they both mean. There certainly was for me when I first started researching them for my own mental health and wellness journey.

If you type in either 'wellness' or 'wellbeing' into a browser, you will often be met with a picture of a beautiful toothy, smiley person eating an apple, or perhaps an image of a runner, a set of weights or a spa massage – everything tends to be pushing towards nutrition, exercise and relaxation.

Now, I am not saying that these elements are not fundamental in both wellness and wellbeing; to make it clear, nutrition, exercise and relaxation should be the foundation of everyone's self-care, but wellness and wellbeing both cover so much more than simply these things. After all, if life was as simple as eating well and exercising more, Gym Bunnies across the world who eat well would never suffer with stress, anxiety, depression, or a multitude of other physical and mental health conditions.

Sadly, I don't think that is the case; in fact, I know it is not, as many of my clients live a very healthy lifestyle when it comes to diet and exercise but still experience mental health issues.

A study of 1.2 million people in the USA found that people who exercise reported having only 1.5 fewer days of poor mental health a month compared to people who do not exercise, which is not the huge difference that many people are led to believe. It also found that more exercise was not always better either, with the study identifying that exercising for 45 minutes three to five times a week was associated with the biggest mental health benefits. Any further exercise after this was found to offer no additional benefits. The study included all types of physical activity, ranging from childcare, housework, lawn-mowing and fishing to cycling, going to the gym, running and skiing. What has been confirmed is that exercise reduces the risk of cardiovascular disease, stroke, diabetes, and mortality from all causes, but its association with mental health remains unclear.

So, to confirm...again...nutrition and activity are the foundation for a positive and healthy life, but they are not wellbeing and wellness in its entirety.

So, what is? The answer to this lies in history, because wellness and wellbeing are not new concepts. It may sometimes feel as if wellness and wellbeing as ideals have been created in the modern world as a direct response to the stressful and chaotic lives the modern approach has brought upon us all, but the fact remains the same: these concepts are not new, and they are not modern. This is, in fact, an ancient belief system that can be found as part of every core religion with a focus on balance and harmony of the spirits, body and mind, dating back to the Bronze Age.

I love a bit of history because our past explains to us our present, and our present gives us an indication of our future. I am a firm believer that we should respect those that came before us, the world they created for us, and we should learn as much as we can. With regards to wellness and wellbeing, we look to where it all began – with philosophy. In the sixth century, philosophy was used as a way of making sense of the world via non-religious approaches, focusing on topics such as mathematics, biology, astronomy, metaphysics, logic ethics and biology, to name a few.

The concept of wellness and wellbeing developed from the philosophies of medicine into the practices of Ayurveda, which roughly translated as 'the knowledge of life'. It was a pseudoscience and an alternative medicine system used over 3,000 years ago in one of my favourite places (and where I spent my honeymoon), India, and it was the foundation of the four sacred texts of Hindu.

Ayurveda is based on the concept that illness develops when the three doshas, *Vata, Pitta and Kapha*, are out of balance; they are the three energies that define a person's makeup. The healing process for Ayurveda is to rebalance the doshas through tools and practices such as medicinal herbs, massage oils, yoga, sweat baths and meditation.

It was not just the people of India who were focusing on wellness and wellbeing – Greek philosophers argued that illness came from poor lifestyle choices. This was then adopted by the Romans, who passed it on to the Europeans when they invaded, and the Europeans then passed it on to the Americans, and so it goes on. With so much travel and translation over the millennia, it is not surprising that the concepts and terminology of wellness and wellbeing can be confused, and in many cases are used interchangeably, leaving us to wonder what it all really means.

When I started my own research, I found myself being drawn to ancient China, where wellness practice was implemented within ancient Chinese culture at the same time as in Egypt, the Middle East, Greece and other countries. But along with the wellness and wellbeing strategies already mentioned, the ancient Chinese also developed the first system of medicine from practices linked to Buddhism and Taoism, such as acupuncture. And it is this link that we start to develop what wellness and wellbeing really means in the modern world, because according to the ancient Chinese, it simply translates as health and happiness.

Wellness translates as 'healthy' or 'nurturing life'. This relates primarily to our physical state, which, to complicate things a little further, can also be affected by our mental, emotional and spiritual state. We start to understand a little more about the concept of balance between more than one state as we understand how all states are affected by each other. The primary focus of wellness is prevention in order to protect our long-term mental and physical health.

Wellbeing translates as 'happiness' or 'a sense of blessedness'. This refers to our mental, emotional and spiritual state; and again, just to complicate things, our mental, emotional and spiritual states are also affected by our physical health. Wellness and wellbeing are very much interlinked, but the core focus of wellbeing is happiness and having a positive existence that incorporates harmony, calm, contentment and balance.

It was from the Chinese concepts of wellness and wellbeing that I started to gain a better understanding of my own wellness and wellbeing too.

I would read everything I could about wellness and wellbeing when I was stuck on trains travelling across the UK, and the concept of balance was the one thing that kept sticking out. It became clear to me that there was no one way to manage my wellness and wellbeing, or for you to manage your wellness and wellbeing. To be healthy, I had to become happy, and to become happy, I had to become healthy. I don't mind telling you my starting point was neither healthy nor happy – it was miserable and sick. Looking back now, I think being stuck on daily commuter trains from Liverpool to Ledbury or Liverpool to Cardiff was not helping with that. I decided to use those five- or sometimes seven-hour round train trips to dig a bit deeper and gain more understanding of my wellness and wellbeing.

I learned wellness and wellbeing are entwined, and this had, in some cases, caused confusion, not just for me but for a lot of people. I accepted then as I do now that they are entwined, but the emphasis should be on how they are entwined – how does our wellness affect our wellbeing and vice versa? The easiest way to demonstrate this is with the concept of stress, something that we all experience at one time or another in life.

As I explained in my 'meaning of life' theory, humans have an in-built system that uses stress to manage our fight or flight response, which boosts our survival and long-term evolution. In my opinion, our stress triggers are our superhero abilities that help us get out of danger. In fact, based on everything we covered about stress, it would be easy to think that stress must be a brilliant thing to experience, right? Wrong, well, at least wrong for many, because when stress becomes unmanageable and overwhelming, it is anything but a good thing; in fact it, can become a very dangerous thing. In high quantities, stress is no longer our survival mechanism: it becomes our kryptonite and can affect both our wellness and our wellbeing. With this in mind, if we are built for it and it supercharges us against adverse danger – where does it all go wrong?

The common understanding of stress is that it is *'a state of mental or emotional strain or tension resulting from adverse or demanding circumstances',* but to help with clarity, I want you to think of stress as taking a nice hot bubble bath.

Imagine you have a bath tub; it normally has a filter or drain hole just beneath the tap (or 'faucet', as my American friends say) and as long as the water is able to be filtered out it will stay at the right level for you to have an amazingly relaxing bath. But if the water becomes too much for the filter to manage, then the water keeps rising and rising. Eventually it rises over the edge of the bathtub and onto the floor, damaging the bathroom, and it then breaks through the floor into other rooms below and damages your entire home.

This is exactly how stress works too. The water represents the stress, the tap represents your life events and circumstances, the things you can't switch off because that is the nature of life (hence the concept that 90% of life happens to you and 10% is just how you react to it), and the filter represents your stress management techniques. The fight or flight response system manages the water pressure, so the more circumstances or events that cause you stress, the faster the water flows into the bathtub. If you don't learn to manage stress and filter it out, just like with an overflowing bathtub, you can damage other areas of your home, or in this case, your life.

Stress can impact many parts of your life, your relationships, job and career, as well as your overall wellness and wellbeing, putting your own survival at risk, thus making it one of the most dangerous obstacles humans have to face. You need to understand it, you need to learn to manage it, and you need to learn to identify it early enough to protect your longer-term wellness and wellbeing.

To help you with that, let's start with understanding it.

As previously stated, stress is '*a state of mental or emotional strain or tension resulting from adverse or demanding circumstances*'.

It is caused by two factors: External stress and internal stress.

1. **External stressors** are those things that happen to us, such as major life changes, work, relationship difficulties, financial issues, workload, children and family.

2. **Internal stressors** are those that happen because of our conditioned mind. The conditioned mind is a set

of standard thoughts that we have learned and developed over time or been taught to anticipate because of our own experience or the experience of others. Examples include an inability to accept uncertainty and the need to always feel in control, a pessimistic outlook, negative self-talk and self-belief, unrealistic expectation of self and others, and the need for perfectionism.

 Because stress is a response to something, we know it can either start in the mind, triggering thoughts and feelings and then physical and behavioural responses, or it can be triggered through physical stress, such as an illness, disability and physical trauma.

Your ability to manage stress lies in the communication that takes place between the prefrontal cortex of the brain (which is responsible for making all decisions) and the hippocampus (which is responsible for providing the support information to make those decisions with). Providing the communication between these two remains intact with no alarming danger zones, you can manage stress effectively. But if the communication between the prefrontal cortex and the hippocampus signals a potential danger, it triggers off the amygdala. This acts like a fire alarm in your head, screeching at you until the danger is controlled and you are safe again. It is a life-saving function. But I also like to think of the amygdala as a teenager having a tantrum; I often refer to it as 'Amy G'. When 'Amy G' senses danger, the response (*imagine screaming, shouting, stamping of feet, slamming doors etc*) leads to a physical reaction throughout the body and an inability for the prefrontal cortex and hippocampus to communicate as effectively (*after all, who could think straight if they were surrounded by a screaming teenager in the midst of a tantrum*). If the stress levels remain at a level we can manage, then eventually 'Amy G' calms down and normality is restored. But if the stress levels of the person increase over the levels they can handle (also known as resilience) 'Amy G' turns from being a functioning teenager with the odd tantrum to a dysfunctional teenager with ongoing issues. We call this the dysfunctional stress cycle, which occurs in five stages:

1. **The life event:** Something stressful occurs that triggers the fight or flight response.

2. **Negative thoughts:** This triggers a negative thinking cycle.

3. **Negative emotions:** The negative thoughts then trigger negative feelings, which then creates a loop between negative thinking and feelings; this is sometimes experienced as anxiety.

4. **Physical symptoms:** The fear from the fight or flight response creates a physical reaction in the body, leading to a wide range of symptoms.

5. **Behaviours:** As a result of the negative thinking, feelings and symptoms, we may begin to behave out of the ordinary, which then may lead to a new stressful life event, starting the cycle all over again.

Examples of each of these are:

Life event: You have a bad day at work, which may be one of many bad days at work but this particular one pushes you over the edge of the cycle of stress from functional to dysfunctional.

Negative thinking: You may start to think you hate your job, you may think you are not good at your job or that you are not liked in your job.

Negative feelings: This may lead to feeling angry, frustrated, sad, inferior, worthless, useless, bullied, isolated, anxious.

Physical symptoms: You may notice headaches, tiredness and a change in appetite.

Behaviour: You may decide to open a bottle of wine, or two, when you get home, to start feeling better again, which may lead to a hangover and a groggy head the next day.

The order may not always be exactly as listed; for example, those who are more somatic may notice their physical symptoms first rather than the emotions and thoughts.

The cycle then begins again with a new life event occurring as a result of the previous one. You may now experience another bad day at work because you are not at your best and your senses are heightened due to your dysfunctional stress. This triggers a new set of negative thoughts, feelings and symptoms leading to behaviours out of your ordinary. The cycle then goes over and over and over until you learn to identify the signs and symptoms of your stress and take back control of it, forcing the cycle back from a dysfunctional stress cycle to a functional one. I like to call it 'the hamster wheel of hell', because you are going round and round and round on a big wheel of overwhelming feelings, thoughts and negativity. My personal hamster wheel of hell was so bad it literally felt that the world was closing in on me, that I was going to be squashed by the walls around me, as if trapped in the labyrinth – it is a moment in my life I will never forget.

The symptoms of our stress lead us to a further understanding of wellness and wellbeing, as they affect both our health and happiness in a wide range of ways. These fall into four core categories: emotional, physical, behavioural and psychological.

Emotional

We know that stress is defined as an emotional tension or mental strain, and it is a common feeling for many people in the modern world. If you have experienced stress, you may have also experienced the emotional symptoms of stress such as:

- feeling out of control
- lack of motivation
- anger and/or frustration
- lack of confidence
- lack of self-esteem
- irritability
- mood swings
- extra sensitivity to criticism
- defensiveness
- feeling tearful.

Physical

If you want to be able to manage and control your stress, the first step is to know the symptoms of your stress. Everyone responds a little differently, so the way I respond may not be the way you or a friend responds. We are all so used to experiencing stress in one way or another that we don't necessarily identify the symptoms when they first start, and so we may miss the emotional symptoms. But because the fight or flight response is triggered through stress, our body physically reacts to it, providing us with a wide range of new symptoms to help us identify our stress levels and take control of them. Some of these symptoms are:

- aches/pains
- muscle tension
- grinding teeth
- frequent colds/infections
- hyperventilating
- feeling like you have a lump in your throat
- frequent pins and needles
- dizziness
- palpitations
- panic attacks/nausea
- physical tiredness
- menstrual changes
- loss of libido/sexual problems.

Behaviour

It is possible to miss the emotional symptoms, and many of the physical symptoms could be misunderstood as side effects of other things happening in our life, so it is possible to miss them too. But you have another chance to identify them, when they start to affect your behaviour in ways such as:

- social withdrawal
- relationship problems
- insomnia or tiredness
- recklessness
- aggression
- nervousness
- increased lying
- prone to accidents
- forgetfulness
- increased reliance on alcohol, smoking, caffeine or drugs
- becoming a workaholic
- poor time management
- poor standards of work.

Psychological

If all of these things are happening to your mind and body, leading you to behave in ways out of the ordinary, then it is no doubt going to affect your psychological state too. In fact, the limbic system completely hijacks the frontal lobes and leads to an inability to reason with stress or the trigger to the stress.

The psychological symptoms of stress include but are not limited to:

- inability to concentrate or make simple decisions
- excessive worrying
- negative thinking
- depression and anxiety
- memory lapses
- vagueness
- being easily distracted
- feeling less intuitive and creative.

The effects of the emotional, physical, behavioural and psychological symptoms on the body and mind are vast and can lead to long-term mental and physical issues.

Brain and nerves: You may have headaches, lack of energy, sadness, nervousness, anger, irritability, trouble concentrating, memory issues and difficulty sleeping. This may lead to a wide range of mental health disorders such as anxiety, panic attacks and depression.

Heart: Your heartbeat becomes faster, leading to palpitations. It increases blood pressure, putting you at risk of heart attack, high cholesterol and stroke.

Stomach and Pancreas: You may feel increased levels of nausea and stomach aches as the digestive system starts to work differently. With the increase of the chemical cortisol (the stress hormone in the body), insulin levels can spike, causing weight gain, changing appetite and increasing the risk of diabetes.

Intestines: Because the digestion process has started to change, you may suffer with diarrhoea, constipation, other digestive issues such as irritable bowel syndrome (IBS) and rapid weight loss. This can stop someone wanting to leave the house, leading to isolation and potential agoraphobia.

Reproductive Organs: For women, this can lead to irregular and painful periods, and for men, impotence and/or low sperm production. A reduced sexual desire and an inability to reproduce can potentially lead to mental health issues, such as depression.

And, if that is not enough, stress also affects us physically through skin problems and muscle aches, especially around the neck, shoulders, arms and upper back where we tend to hold onto tension. It can also lead to low bone density and a weakened immune system.

These symptoms and long-term issues caused by stress show the link between our mind and body. If one is affected or injured, it is most likely that the other will be too. Our mental health affects our physical health, and our physical health affects our mental health, and so it is important to be able to manage and care for them both. Mental health and physical health, health and happiness, wellness and wellbeing are pairings that have been part of our biological makeup since the evolution of humans and will continue to be so for a long time to come. It is therefore important that we start to understand the true meaning of wellness and wellbeing to be able to detect when one or both might be affected. We are then able to implement strategies to counteract any negative experiences that could lead to any wellness and wellbeing deterioration, so we are able to protect both our longer-term metal and physical health.

Since the ancient Egyptians, Greeks and Chinese originally learnt the connection between health and happiness and developed and implemented wellness and wellbeing into ancient cultures and religious practice, wellness and wellbeing have since been developed further.

In 1961, Halbert L. Dunn published *High-Level Wellness*, which became the foundation of the wellness movement from the eighties. In the book, Dunn distinguished between good health (not being ill) and what he termed 'high-level wellness', which he defined as '*a condition of change in which the individual moves forward, climbing toward a higher potential of functioning*'. He also promoted the idea that there was more to health simply than the absence of disease. His concepts did not make a big impact for over a decade until they were picked up by other wellness leaders and have since become embedded into popular culture, making these ideas a huge part of our modern lives.

So, thanks to the ancient Egyptians, Greeks, Romans, Chinese, Europeans, Americans and basically every culture across the planet, wellness and wellbeing are understood to be an important part of human existence. This is why it is important that you understand the difference between the two, and most importantly, are able to identify when your wellness and wellbeing are in danger. This means understanding your mind and your body enough to be able to identify when there is no longer a positive balance between your health and happiness and knowing what steps to take in order to restore that balance and protect your longer-term mental and physical health.

It is also important to understand the full spectrum of wellness so that you are able to implement self-care plans that are effective in improving your overall wellness and wellbeing and not fall into the trap of following everyone else and just doing what everyone else does. You are unique. Your life journey is unique to you, and so to follow others on the path to your own wellness and wellbeing will lead to bumps in the road and frustrations that can hold you back with longer-term detrimental effects.

In theory, improving your wellness and wellbeing to protect your mental and physical health could not be easier, as there are so many options available to you. At the click of a button, you can access wellness assessments, health checks, gym classes, courses, retreats, online coaching, therapy, books, TV shows and podcasts. The key, however, is identifying your own symptoms and developing a tool belt of the most effective ways to manage your wellness and wellbeing from all the options available to you, and perhaps even creating some for yourself.

What I learnt on those long train journeys, listening to endless audio books whilst staring out the window at the stunning Herefordshire countryside, is that as populations grow and we live longer, we have a responsibility to manage our wellness and wellbeing in order to not only protect our own health and happiness but also the healthcare systems and social systems that try to protect our communities. The more effort each of us puts in to staying healthy, happy, and stress-free, the better everyone will be as a result, because our communities and society as a whole will also be healthier and happier too.

To summarise, in a nutshell, what does wellness and wellbeing mean? The key themes between them both are balance, prevention and lifestyle choices that improve and protect your physical and mental health. By practicing wellness and wellbeing, you lead a better life. You are less stressed, you enjoy life more, and you have more energy to do the things you want to do, in turn making you happier and healthier.

Simply put. it's all about the H's – health and happiness. When thinking about wellness, think 'health', and when thinking about wellbeing, think 'happiness'. Remember, one does not function effectively without the other – which means you do not function healthily or happily without both. It is for this reason I recommend you start implementing your own wellness and wellbeing strategy with a little 8Wise guidance, and start investing in yourself, your wellness, your wellbeing and your longer-term health and happiness. In fact, you're already taking the first step by reading this book.

Make your lifestyle all about the two W's, wellness and wellbeing, and the H's, health and happiness, and become as wise (or, as you'll soon learn, as '8Wise') as the ancient peoples of Greece, China, and India.

Chapter 4:

Traumas and Triggers

When I started my coaching and therapy business, I decided to throw myself into the world of networking. I was petrified. I am not comfortable walking up to strangers in a large busy room and just 'selling'. It's not me, and in those early days of my business, I was in awe of those that could sell; so, I thought I would do what I do best: observe from the side lines and learn how to do it from those that were doing it well.

Eventually, just like I had done as a child when debating my big questions with the people I felt comfortable with, I soon started to feel comfortable in the breakfast meetings at 6:30am on a Friday morning at the Marriott Hotel. I also became more at ease at the after-work drinks on busy Castle Street in Liverpool. I began to find myself discussing and sharing my understanding and knowledge of mental health, stress, anxiety, depression, burnout and low self-esteem, to name just a few of my favourite topics *(as you can see, I am such fun at a dinner party)*, and my new network started to show interest. This then led to an invitation for me to be a guest speaker at an event for fifty business people to explain what my company, Dalton Wise, did. This is what I said …

'Dalton Wise is the one-stop shop for learning to manage your gun.'

Now, as you can imagine, their faces were a picture of confusion – after all, what on Earth does mental health have to do with guns? – so I explained my analogy.

What makes a gun dangerous? Is it when someone pulls the trigger? Or is it when someone puts the bullet inside of it and *then* pulls the trigger? The answer is the latter, because without the bullet, a gun is just a solid, shiny, empty metal carcass.

Now imagine that the gun represents your mental health, the trigger of the gun represents your current stress levels, and the bullet represents all of the past traumas and experiences that you have stored in your subconscious.

Through a therapeutic coaching approach (which is how I work with my clients), I focus on the 'past, present, future' approach.

I first start with the present, supporting someone to build up the resilience and develop the coping skills to manage their stress, anxiety or depression. This prevents them from pulling the trigger on their mental health gun, now or in the future. This approach reduces the danger level of the gun. *Gun analogy, stage one.*

But we have to be aware that a gun remains dangerous whilst there are still bullets inside it. There may be times when the stress levels are simply too much and so the trigger is pressed, releasing the bullet, which in this case could be anything from childhood traumas, early adult traumas or recent supressed traumas.

Whilst the bullet still stays inside a gun, the gun remains a dangerous object, just like if unprocessed traumas still exist, then there is always a risk to your mental health. So, to reduce the danger levels, we need to remove the bullet. We therefore need to unlock the subconscious memories and work through the traumas and past experiences, because a processed trauma equals low to no risk, like a blank unharmful bullet. *Gun analogy, stage two.*

Now, if only life was kind and only ever gave us one bullet, one trauma, or one tragic event, but it doesn't – we can experience traumas and tragedy throughout our life and so we can always access more bullets in the future. Therefore, a therapeutic coaching approach also needs to not only work through the traumas of the past and develop the tools to manage the stress of the present, but it also needs to prepare you or support you to manage the traumas of the future. In life, we need to accept that we will always need to remove bullets from our gun if we don't want to keep firing them. *Gun analogy, stage three.*

What I was trying to explain to that group of stressed-out business people with my gun analogy, and what I am trying to explain to you now, is that life is always about traumas and triggers; it's always about managing the dangers and lowering the risks, and that's what keeps us healthy, mentally and physically. We can't always do this on our own: sometimes we need some support to be able to identify signs and symptoms, know when to manage the triggers and when to process the traumas so we can stay on track towards positive mental health.

Your Mind

Your mind is a powerful thing; according to psychologists through the ages, it is the most powerful part of the human body. It is often confused with the brain, but they are two very different things. Your brain is the physical organ, and your mind is the neurological transcendent world of thought, feeling, attitude, belief and imagination. If you want to get spiritual about it, it could be argued that your mind is where your soul lies, but I will let you make your own mind up about that.

Although the mind may start within the brain, it is not confined to it; in fact, the intelligence of your mind permeates every cell of your body, not just brain cells, and so your mind has tremendous power over all of your bodily systems. This is why when you feel stress, you feel it mentally and physically, because stress is triggered by your mind.

Each experience you have in life is stored in a different place within your mind. There are slightly different psychological thoughts on this, but as this is not a psychology textbook, I am sharing the one I heavily lean to the most, which says there are three different parts of your mind:

- Conscious mind
- Subconscious mind
- Unconscious mind.

The concept of the conscious and unconscious mind was developed from the work of Sigmund Freud (1915), and through the years as psychology evolved, the concept of the subconscious mind was added.

The human mind is like an iceberg – the most important part of the mind is the part you cannot see, the part that lies right underneath the water. It is only our conscious mind that sits above the water – our subconscious and unconscious minds sit firmly beneath the water and are the primary source of human behaviour.

Freud argued that our feelings, motives and decisions are powerfully influenced by our past experiences which are stored in the unconscious mind, driving and guiding us through life. I remember connecting to this concept quite powerfully when I first listened to a lecture about it. It brought great personal clarity, self-acceptance and understanding, as if I suddenly made sense to myself, and it has since influenced my own professional work, as explained previously in my gun analogy, because the subconscious and unconscious mind are what connect the trigger to the bullet.

But what makes up the human mind? What really lies above and below the water in the iceberg analogy?

1. Your **Conscious mind** makes up 10% of your available mind. It consists of accessible and available information such as your will power, thoughts and perceptions. It is where your decision-making processes take place as well as your logical thinking and your initial learning process. Anything stored in

your conscious mind is like having an open Word document on your computer – it remains open until you have finished your work on it and are ready to save and close it.

2. Your **Subconscious mind** makes up 50% of your available mind. It is much deeper than your conscious mind and is less accessible. It is where you experience reoccurring thoughts, and it is also where your behaviours, habits, feelings and knowledge are stored. Recent memories are also filtered into your subconscious mind. Anything stored in your subconscious mind is like a saved and closed Word document on your computer.

3. Your **Unconscious mind** makes up the final 40% of your available mind. It stores all your early childhood memories, beliefs and habits. This includes traumatic events, phobias, addictions, urges, selfish needs, shameful experiences and violent motives. Any information that is needed to resist change or override your other two minds is stored here. Your unconscious mind is 'you'; it is your life in full – every experience exists within this part of your mind. Anything stored in your unconscious mind is like having an archived document on your computer.

Since birth, you have been collecting all the memories linked to the life experiences you have had, and they all go towards helping you with your core purpose which, as I have explained previously, I believe is to 'survive and evolve'.

Your mind filters the experiences into the part of itself that it thinks the information is best stored in. If it is a current learning process, for example, it will remain in your conscious mind until a time when that learning has become knowledge, then it will be moved and stored in your subconscious mind.

Let's look at that example in a little more detail with regards to learning to read.

- When you first start to learn to read, you process the learning in your conscious mind, and so from the perspective of the computer analogy, your document stays open.

- When you have learned to read and the learning becomes embedded knowledge that you need to access moving forward, it moves from your conscious mind to your subconscious mind, and from the perspective of the computer analogy, it becomes a saved document.

For example, if for some reason you struggled to learn to read – if it took you longer or you experienced a learning difficulty that was undiagnosed in your early years – you may have developed strong feelings towards reading, such as shame, anger or phobia, and these get stored in your unconscious mind; not easily accessible but always there and just simply archived.

This process takes place for all learning experiences, traumatic ones and even the ones you think are not important or you may have forgotten about. Your mind has all of them stored either as a memory, a belief, a feeling, a thought, a behaviour, a habit, or a fear, and if what is stored in your unconscious mind are traumas, when triggered these can affect your mental health greatly. With regards to the gun analogy, everything in your unconscious mind can be activated as a bullet if triggered by a new or current experience – the present can awaken the past and affect the future.

What Are Traumas?

The power of the mind is demonstrated through the process of trauma. There are many descriptions of trauma, but this is the one I find to be most helpful:

Trauma is any event or experience that overwhelms the brain's ability to cope, and shapes our beliefs or behaviours going forward. (Treatment Improvement Protocol (TIP) Series, No. 57. 2014)

It can be understood even more simply if we look at trauma as anything that causes us deep, lasting distress during or after the traumatic event has taken place. What this really means is that trauma is less about *what happened to us* and much more about *our perception* and subjective emotional experience of the traumatic event. This is why trauma is unique to the individual, and how the experience of one event may impact two people in different ways.

Trauma can happen at any stage in our lives, and it can leave you struggling with upsetting emotions, memories, and anxiety that won't go away. It can also leave you feeling numb, disconnected, and unable to trust other people.

Often, but not always, a traumatic experience can involve a threat to our life or our safety, but any situation that leaves you feeling overwhelmed and isolated can result in trauma, even if it doesn't involve physical harm. The more frightened and helpless you feel, the more likely you are to be traumatised.

Trauma can be very complex, and so it is broken into three types:

Acute Trauma: This is often a single incident that occurs at any stage in life, such as if you are in an accident, if you have ever been the victim of a crime or experienced a natural disaster. You may have experienced one of these in the past and find yourself still trying to make sense of it now. The symptoms of acute trauma may include:

- severe panic or extreme anxiety
- confusion and/or irritation
- dissociation or feelings of being disconnected from one's self and their surroundings
- insomnia
- suspiciousness or acting in strange ways
- lack of self-care and poor grooming
- loss of focus or production at work or school.

Chronic Trauma: This often occurs when you experience multiple prolonged overwhelming traumatic situations, such as treatment for illness, or sometimes in situations when you have simply suffered one unrelated trauma after another. People who work in frontline services like the police, paramedics or combat service can be exposed to situations that could lead to chronic trauma. The symptoms of chronic trauma are different to those of acute trauma, as they may not come to the surface for a very long time. Some longer-term reactions to trauma can include:

- unpredictable emotions
- flashbacks
- anxiety
- rage
- physical symptoms like fatigue, headaches or nausea.

Complex Trauma: This trauma commonly occurs with repeated trauma against a child or adult and often involves an invasive experience of an interpersonal nature. These events are incredibly damaging. Situations that can cause complex trauma include all forms of child abuse, neglect, adverse childhood experiences, community violence, domestic and family violence, civil unrest, war trauma or genocide, cultural dislocation, sexual exploitation and trafficking. As well as feelings of anger, sadness and despair, the symptoms for complex trauma can include:

- distrust
- suicidal thoughts
- isolation guilt, shame or feeling different to others
- helpless and hopelessness
- self-harm and self-mutilation
- alcoholism and other substance abuse.

It is important to understand if there may be some traumatic experiences stored in your subconscious mind. You need to be aware of the symptoms and identify if you are experiencing them. If you are, then my recommendation is to see a professional who can support you to work through them. It's the first step to removing that dangerous bullet.

You don't have to have experienced extreme trauma to have your mental health triggered, so it's equally important to understand what triggers are.

What Are Triggers?

I recently read a comment left on a post on social media about anxiety. The person had stated how *'one person's panic attack is another person's uncomfortable situation and that the person who has the panic attack should just "get a grip" and stop being weak'.* I find it uncomfortable when those who experience mental health issues are labelled as weak in some way. Mental health is not as simple as being either mentally strong or mentally weak; a lot of it is about primal and instinctive responses to what we perceive to be dangerous, and that develops from our own life experiences. As we all have different life experiences, we all have different dangers we instinctively react to. Just because someone responds differently to you does not make them weaker or stronger than you, it simply means the dangers that trigger their responses are different to the dangers that trigger yours. In my opinion, unless you have access to the intense training that helps a person change these automatic responses, which is not something most people have access to, it is dangerous for anyone to be under the illusion that they have control over their immediate responses to a situation. Because the fact of the matter is none of us have an immediate control over our automatic responses because they are primitive, engrained in us as part of our biological makeup; they are instinctive and not conscious, they are a process, not an ability. To understand this and show empathy to those experiencing mental health issues triggered through their primitive response is a huge step in tackling the stigma of mental health.

Our fight or flight mode is a survival instinct; it is an active defence response, an automatic reaction, and it isn't a conscious thought, so neither you nor I can control it *(without a lot of intense training)*. All we can do is understand why we respond the way we do to a specific trigger and take control of the situation as soon as we feel the symptoms of the response in order to reduce its impact. Part of that process is learning what triggers you.

Triggers are events or circumstances that may produce very uncomfortable emotional or psychiatric symptoms, such as anxiety, panic, discouragement, despair, or negative self-talk. They are the experience of having an emotional reaction to some type of disturbing content. They are anything that might cause you to recall a traumatic experience or deep-rooted feelings and thoughts. Reacting to triggers is normal: you are not weak, you are not inferior, you are simply a normal human being.

Although most of us cannot necessarily control the fight or flight response that is triggered, we can learn to manage the event, situation or set of circumstances that triggers it in the first place, and therefore you do have the ability to prevent the response from happening.

Where Do Triggers Come From?

Because we all live a life of different experiences, triggers widely vary from person to person and can be either internal or external.

Internal triggers come from within the person, what I call your internal world, the world that exists inside of you, such as memories, emotions, feelings and physical sensations. For example, a few years ago my dad had a heart attack, so sometimes if I ever feel my heart pounding when I am exercising, it can trigger health anxiety for me, and I then have to manage the symptoms of the anxiety.

Other common internal triggers include pain, muscle tension, memories tied to traumatic events, anger, sadness, loneliness, anxiety, feeling overwhelmed, vulnerable, abandoned, or out of control.

External triggers come from the environment. They can be a person, a place, or a specific situation. For example, also a few years ago I was in a car accident, and so whenever I hear or feel a car slam on its breaks, it triggers an anxiety response, which I then need to manage and prevent from spiralling out of control.

Other things that may cause external triggers are significant dates, specific times of day, a specific location, a movie, television show, or news article, a sight, sound, taste, or smell, a person, changes to a relationship or ending a relationship, arguing with a friend, spouse, or partner.

With so many possible trigger options, why do we get triggered by some things and not by others? The truth is we don't know precisely how triggers are formed. It has been argued that our brains store memories from a traumatic event differently from memories of a non-traumatic event, such as storing past traumatic events as current events, and so if something triggers them you may feel it as if you are experiencing the original trauma all over again.

What we do know is triggers can cause an emotional reaction before you even realise it is happening, and so although you can't necessarily control the response you are having, you can learn to cope with it, as I have learnt to manage and cope with the anxiety I experience.

You may be asking yourself, what has all of this got to do with wellness and wellbeing? Health and happiness? Mental and physical health? Well, in simple terms, the truth is that we will wander through life responding to what it throws at us. Some of those experiences will have a bigger impact on us than others, sometimes negatively but sometimes positively too. We know we can't control our responses to those events in the immediate moment as our survival instinct works a lot quicker than our conscious mind. Therefore, all we can do is learn to manage the symptoms of the response or remove ourselves from situations we know will trigger a negative response. In order to do this, we need to understand all of the triggers and responses we have, the impact they have and the situation or set of circumstances that trigger them in the first place – this this is what improving your wellness and wellbeing means, and this is what 8Wise will help you to do.

Learning to Manage Traumas and Triggers

The main thing I have learnt through my own mental health journey, personal development and self-discovery is that it doesn't matter what your belief system in life is, whether you lean towards philosophical, religious or scientific debate. Where the questions come from really doesn't matter because when it comes down to your mental health the answer is always traumas and triggers.

Whether you choose to use philosophical, religious or medical approaches, when it comes down to it, all approaches for mental health diagnostics, care and recovery, are about trying to manage the triggers and traumas. So, to improve your wellness and wellbeing, you need to identify all of the things that put you at risk, whether that be mentally or physically. This means all of the life experiences and events that trigger both an emotional and physical reaction in you or a set of symptoms that have an impact on your mental and physical health negatively. You then need to counteract them with actions that reduce their impact.

To improve your wellbeing, you need to be able to implement a strategy for managing and coping with the events that life throws at you, those that cause you stress and impact on your mental health. You need to create experiences that have more positive reactions and triggers to reduce the impact of negative ones.

You need to do this for the rest of your life to manage your wellness and wellbeing effectively, and it all starts with understanding your body, understanding your mind and understanding the life you have lived to date and the impact it has had on you.

And finally, welcome to 8Wise, your tool for improving your wellness and protecting your longer-term mental and physical health for a happier, healthier and more fulfilled life. A model that focuses on understanding your triggers and traumas and how to manage them whether they be from your past, your present or your future.

Or in other words, how to remove the bullets from a very dangerous gun.

PART TWO

The 8Wise Way

Chapter 5:

An Introduction to 8Wise

What is 8Wise?

8Wise is the only model you will ever need for managing your mental wellbeing. It consists of four core wellness dimensions, each broken into two wellness elements that create the eight focus points for the model (hence the '8' in 8Wise). The focus points help you to breakdown your overall wellness into eight manageable chunks so you can manage your wellness and wellbeing, not just for now, but for the rest of your life. The 8Wise model supports you in developing the knowledge, skills and tools (the 'Wise' part of 8Wise) to improve your wellness and to protect your mental and physical health for a happier and healthier life.

How do I use it?

Through the remaining chapters of this book, I will be taking you through the same process I share with my private clients in two phases: knowledge and action.

Phase One: The Knowledge Phase

This provides you with the underpinning knowledge of each 8Wise core dimension and element, so you can understand the psychology and science behind it and how it impacts your wellness and wellbeing. It also provides you with the **information** needed for you to assess yourself against each core dimension and create a tailored action plan for achieving your wellness and wellbeing goals with the support of the action phase.

Phase Two: The Action Phase

This provides you with the **tools** to assess your 8Wise wellness levels and set some tangible goals. It also provides you with some tools and techniques to help you develop a realistic action plan to meet those goals.

I believe there is more than one way to get the most out of this book, and they cater for two types of people:

1. Person A: who likes to read through everything in order first, before moving onto the action phase

2. Person B: who likes to jump ahead to the bits that interest them most.

The good news is that you can choose either option as long as you move from phase one to phase two for each dimension and element. No matter which way you choose to use this book, you will come away with a tangible action plan that will improve your wellness and wellbeing.

- If you are person A, simply follow each of the chapters in order along with all activities.

- If you are person B, just follow the page number prompts at the end of each chapter.

Simply grab a notebook and pen and start making some notes.

Or if you have an 8Wise Journal, you can use that too.

Welcome to Your Own 8Wise™ Wellness Journey

Like with all journeys, we have a destination in place, and although many of you will have different ideas about your preferred destination, they no doubt link to your longer-term mental and physical health in one way or another. With all journeys, we have a starting place, and your 8Wise journey starts with 'home'.

What Does Home Mean to You?

I believe that home means a secure, cheerful, happy place where you are respected and loved, and where you can live, laugh and learn freely as your true self.

I learnt this from a ten-year-old named Wyn, from British Colombia in Canada, who wrote an essay about what does 'home' mean to him for an essay writing competition. The question was put to students in Grades 4, 5 and 6 nationwide, and Wyn was one of two finalists sharing his thoughts on the meaning of 'home'.

What does home really mean to me? To me, home means not one, but many things. Most importantly, I believe that home means a secure, cheerful place where you are respected and loved. But what about the people without homes? Does it mean the same thing to them? Everybody deserves to know the true meaning of home. When I started writing this essay, I didn't think much about the meaning of home. But now, I have found out that home means more. Much more.

Home means an enjoyable, happy place where you can live, laugh and learn. It's somewhere where you are loved, respected, and cared for. When you look at it from the outside, home is just a house. A building. Maybe a yard. But on the inside, it's a lot more than wood and bricks. The saying "Home is where the heart is" says it all.

I have never met Wyn and may never have the privilege to do so. I simply stumbled across his story when researching wellness and it stuck with me because after reading his story I understood my own preoccupation with buying a house, and my fixation on it bringing me safety and security. But what I really 'craved' was a 'home', and I had never really thought about why a home is important until Wyn's fabulous essay opened my eyes. It was then I started to realise that what was really at the heart of my 'fixation'; what I was really looking for was a safe place to be me, a secure place to be me, somewhere I could let my guard down, feel free to be unapologetically myself – what I was yearning for was a home.

That realisation made me think about the fact that although not everyone necessarily has a 'home', it is possibly the one thing that we are really all striving for, the one desire we all have in common. After all, the saying is 'home is where the heart is', and our heart is a pretty big deal in keeping us alive and our 'home' is an important factor in making us feel alive, or at least safe and secure.

Abraham Harold Maslow's paper 'A Theory of Human Motivation', published in 1943, described the well-known Maslow's Hierarchy of Needs. Maslow's work had been following me throughout my professional life, as a university student studying criminology, as a designer and developer of community and corporate training courses and then as a psychotherapist. I have always felt it to be a good model for understanding the commonality between all humans when so many other things focus on our differences. And when I started to think more and more about the concept of 'home', I found myself being drawn towards Maslow's work once more.

Although Maslow's theory is not specifically about the importance of 'home', in his work we can start to see why 'home' is important to us. Maslow proposed that humans have needs that are layered into five levels, and the structure of those needs is hierarchical. He proposes that we move upwards through them but only after completing each level – like in video games, but instead of collecting coins, weapons, money, tricks or fruits etc., you collect life lessons and fulfilment. You can't truly move to the next level, or 'need' until you have fulfilled the one before it. And if you do move up through all of the needs, then you reach utopia – otherwise known as self-actualisation, where you are able to fulfil your full potential. But to get there, you have to start at level one.

Maslow's Hierarchy of Needs

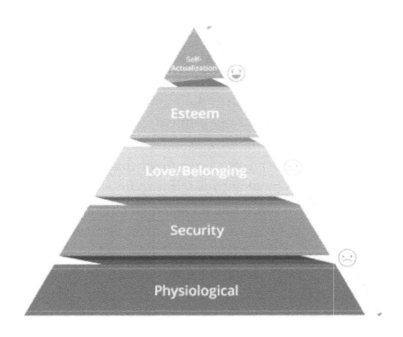

As you can see from the diagram, level one in Maslow's Hierarchy of Needs focuses on our **Physiological Needs**. These are our primary needs as humans and consist of things that are vital for our survival, such as food, water, breathing, sleep, clothes, homeostasis (stable biological systems) and shelter. From my perspective this is the first time that the concept of 'home' enters Maslow's theory of human needs – because the first function of a 'home' is to provide us with shelter, food, water and a place to sleep – it is not just bricks and mortar.

After attaining everything from level one of the Hierarchy of Needs, we move through to level two, which focusses on **Security and Safety Needs**. This links to the security and safety we need in our lives in order to have some control. Again, this also links to the concept of 'home', being a place that provides safety and security. When our 'home' does not provide safety or security, it can affect our stability, our health and wellbeing, and our concept of our self and our self-worth.

After level one, Physiological needs, and level two, Safety and Security needs, you move to the third level of human needs, and this involves feelings of **Love and Belonging**. The need for interpersonal relationships, for intimacy, for trust, acceptance and love. This started me thinking that our level three needs therefore also link to our need for 'home', a safe place where we need to experience feeling loved and cared for by others, enough so that we can grow confidently internally. This enables our self-esteem and self-belief to grow positively, developing and fulfilling our internal safety and security needs for ourselves. This is similar to where Maslow takes us for levels four and five, **Esteem** and **Self-Actualisation**. I am going to leave you to read up on Maslow yourself for further information on those two – it's worth it.

What I took from Maslow is that we don't really pay attention to understanding the needs we have; we just feel them, are driven by them and rely heavily on external sources to fulfil them, which easily leads to blame, shame and anger when that does not happen. In many ways, I feel this is a lot like our house or our home. For me, it can be difficult to see the shell of the house that holds my home together – I trust that others such as builders and construction teams will develop a structure for me that is safe enough to build my home in. The building or the house that provides me with the structure that enables me to create a beautiful home sometimes gets ignored in favour of all the drama I create about the 'things' I choose to put inside of it *(I genuinely once had an epic meltdown over the wrong shade of grout in the bathroom – we call it 'grout gate' in my house).*

If I do start to notice the outside starting to crumble a little, I then entrust someone else to come and fix it for me in order to protect all the things I have collected, created and developed on the inside of it, and I tell myself I do this because I can't do it myself. Someone is better than me at this. I don't have the skills or the tools. I don't know where to start. And that in many ways is true, but what I leave out of the thinking is that I could learn some of those skills, if I choose to, if I want more control over the 'structure', that makes me feel safe, secure and loved.

It is from this philosophical viewpoint that I have identified that maybe we are just like our houses and our homes. It's interesting that when I ask my clients how they are feeling the first time I meet with them; the common answer is *'I feel like I'm falling apart'* or *'I feel life my life is crumbling around me'*. These are words and phrases I used myself when I was in the depths of my own despair. And it is from this commonality of language that I give you my next analogy – you are a house, and you are also your own home.

When we build a house or a home, there are four core levels to it:

The Foundations

This is the part of the house that is developed deep into the ground so that whatever is built on top of it is stable and longstanding. I liken this is to the foundations of our own lives, our fitness, our health and our strength to live the life we want for as long as we can.

The External Structure

This consists of the walls, the roof, the doors and windows of the house. These essential structures and external features not only create safety and security from the elements but also provide us with the enclosed space where we can function effectively. I liken this to the external sources in our lives that keep us safe and secure whilst we transition through all the stages of our life, things like our relationships, educational systems and our professional systems.

The Internal Structure

This consists of all the rooms (kitchen, bathroom, lounge, bedroom) and the spaces we choose to spread out in (attic, basement, cupboards, gardens) that provide us with the ability to function and flow easily throughout our homes. I liken this to our beliefs, thoughts, wants and needs – those things that provide us with the internal dialogue enabling us to interact, react and function within the external world.

The Interior Design

This is the personalisation of the space. It is what takes an empty, dull canvass and changes it into a vibrant, beautiful space, an extension of our own personality through colour, textures and objects. I liken this to the lifestyle we choose to live, the choices we make to achieve our dreams, ambitions and goals and what makes our life fulfilling and happy.

I believe that we have the ability to create the most beautiful life in the same way we have the ability to create the most beautiful home. I am not saying it is easy, I am saying it is possible if you allow yourself to learn the knowledge and skills to do it whilst also believing that you have the ability to do it too.

Going back to what Wyn said earlier

> it's a lot more than wood and bricks. Home is also where your memories lie and also where your hopes and dreams are.

So are you – you are so much more than what you see in the mirror; you are so much more than your perception of what you hear, think and feel. You consist of the biological functions that keep you alive and the psychological responses to your experiences that have shaped your mind. And remember what I said about the mind: it is powerful, it controls every cell in your body. Wouldn't it be great to be able to manage how your mind is trained and use that power to manage life's challenges and transitions more effectively?

Wouldn't it be great to understand how you can build your own strong house and beautiful home? In this analogy, your house represents your wellness, and your home represents your wellbeing, and what I want to help you with is to develop the tools to be able to respond to life rather than react to it, because responding has an element of proactivity, control and management, whereas being reactive is impulsive and chaotic. This can have its place but is not the most productive way to live.

Take the emergency services as an example. They are response units because they have a framework in place that, no matter what emergency may come through, allows them to respond effectively and with reasonable degrees of confidence. And that's what I want for you and what I want to support you with – becoming your own response unit for protecting yourself, with a clear framework of how to respond to anything effectively, even when you have no idea about what might be coming. We can't control what life throws at us, but we can learn to develop a framework to live our lives by which will give us the power to respond in a way that is effective and less damaging.

In my analogy, your body is your house, and everything else about you and your life is your home. I created 8Wise as a framework for building a strong and healthy person who can then create a beautifully long, happy and fulfilling life. Through 8Wise, I want to share with you the tools to develop your own 'house and home' (wellness and wellbeing) and help you to become your own response unit to protect it.

8Wise will help you be your own construction team – are you ready to start building something strong and sustainable that also provides you with flexibility and ability to adapt to the winding roads of life?

Let me make it clear, this is not a one-size-fits-all approach: this is a model, a framework, a formula, this is the house you build your home in – you are the designer, you are the detail. With that premise in mind, 8Wise is a process that can support you to develop a unique response toolkit for managing life's trials and tribulations effectively in order to prevent or reduce any long-term damage to your mental or physical health that life's traumas and triggers may cause.

8Wise is a conscious process leading you to a more satisfying life. This is achieved through defining a wellness and wellbeing balance for yourself and introducing a range of healthy behaviours that support you in achieving that balance. These behaviours should include setting and meeting goals aimed at improving and maintaining a good balance across all eight dimensions of wellness.

8Wise has successfully supported a range of my clients to find their balance, reduce their stress and anxiety, and develop the tools and techniques to not only face their problems, but also find their own solutions too.

The process is simple but incredibly effective and supports the approaches I work best with – goal setting and working towards tangible outcomes, whether it be for personal or professional success.

The following chapters outline how you can use 8Wise to develop a personalised wellness plan, for yourself, which will put you back in control of your wellness and wellbeing in the present and help you to continue managing it moving forward into your future.

Like building a house, the eight areas we will focus on fall into four categories:

Foundation Dimensions

This category consists of the wellness dimensions that, just like a house, give us a strong foundation. Physical wellness involves taking care of your body for optimal health and functioning. Emotional wellness involves having a positive attitude, high self-esteem, a strong sense of self, and the ability to recognise and share a wide range of feelings with others in a constructive way. This category focuses on the baseline for health and happiness.

Internal Dimensions

This category consists of the wellness dimensions that tell us most about ourselves. Spiritual wellness is not about religion, although for some people religion will play a big part in it. It is about finding meaning in life events, identifying and embracing your purpose, and living a life that reflects your values and beliefs. Intellectual wellness involves learning more, being open to new ideas, being creative, thinking critically, and seeking out new challenges. This category focuses on our inner world, who we are and what we want.

External Dimensions

This category consists of the wellness dimensions that affect how we interact with the world. Environmental wellness is about being aware of our interactions between the environment, our community and ourselves, and behaving in ways that care for each of these responsibly. Social wellness involves building relationships with others, dealing with conflict appropriately, and connecting to a positive social network. This category focuses on how we interact with the spaces around us and who we welcome in to share them.

Lifestyle Dimensions

This category consists of the wellness dimensions that help us to develop the life we want for ourselves. Occupational wellness is about seeking to have a career that is interesting, enjoyable, meaningful and that contributes to the larger society. Financial wellness involves living within your means and learning how to manage your finances for the short and long term in order to live a life that brings fulfilment rather than stress. This category focuses on how we build a life and the means to creating our lifestyle of choice.

No matter what your difficulty, problem or challenge in life is, it will be having an effect across all eight dimensions of what I call your wellness spectrum. By using the 8Wise approach you can limit, prevent or reduce the damage that past, present and future traumas and triggers may have. 8Wise will help you to build your own effective response unit for the challenges and transitions you will face in your life that will have an impact on your full wellness spectrum – the eight dimensions of wellness.

In a nutshell, 8Wise is a therapeutic life coaching programme that combines the concepts of psychotherapy and coaching alongside philosophical and scientific discussion for a more effective model to improve wellness and wellbeing as well as manage stress-related issues for the long term.

Chapter 6:

The Foundation Dimensions

Your health and wellbeing is just like a tree: *'When the roots are deep there is no need to fear the wind.' – African Proverb*. This is why we need to have solid foundations and why the 8Wise model begins with the Foundation Dimensions, the two areas of wellness that keep you strong in body and mind – your physical and emotional wellness.

Emotional Wellness

You do not have to be positive or feel happy all of the time – you are a human, after all, not a robot! Emotional wellness is about finding the balance between feeling and expressing emotions effectively in a healthy way and not drowning in them in an unhealthy way that dictates your quality of life. To do this, you need to not only manage your emotions and how you express them but also develop strong self-esteem, with an inner dialogue and conditioned mind which does not negatively affect your quality of life. You know you have secured some balance within this dimension when you have successfully learned to cope effectively with life. When you have emotional wellness, you feel in control of your feelings and confident in yourself and your abilities. You can control your behaviours, and you can handle the challenges occurring throughout your life. Emotional wellness can lead you to develop resilience and an ability to manage and overcome the challenges life will bring you. Your emotional wellness triggers every other area of your wellness spectrum and is also triggered by all of the other areas too, so it is extremely powerful in your health, wellbeing and quality of life.

There is a strong link between mental health and emotional wellness – remember, mental health links to our psychological or emotional health and wellbeing.

Mental health refers to how we think, how we feel, how we behave, how life affects us and how we cope with it, how we engage with others, and the choices we make. If someone has a lot of problems managing their emotions over a long period of time, this is called **emotional dysregulation.** This is a psychological difficulty that affects mental health. Emotional dysregulation is thought to be a big part of mental health problems such as anxiety, depression, personality disorders, psychosis and post-traumatic stress disorder. Fortunately, we can learn to manage our emotions in healthy ways at any stage in our lives. To start with, it can be helpful to learn more about the basics – starting with asking, What are emotions?

Earlier, we discussed the different levels of your mind and how your **Conscious mind** is where your decision-making processes take place, your **Subconscious mind** is where you experience reoccurring thoughts and where your behaviours, habits, feelings and knowledge are stored, and your

Unconscious mind is 'you'. The unconscious mind stores every experience you have ever had – all of your emotions are triggered from here through emotions, feelings and mood.

Time for some clarity, as these three little beauties get confused a lot.

- Emotions are an intense reaction to a specific incident that release a response chemical and last about six seconds. So, we quickly experience the emotion first, like a wave, as a biological response.

- Feelings are the cognitive thinking process of the emotions; it is when we feel both an emotional and physical sensation. So, we experience the emotion and then process it, which triggers a feeling.

- Mood is not necessarily caused by a trigger, it is an underlying feeling, usually negative or positive. Although it can be influenced by a wide range of factors such as your environment, your physiology and your mental state, it is less intense than emotion and feeling, but no less powerful.

Emotions

We have the ability to experience a wide number of emotions, but thanks to the work of Aristotle in the 4th century BC, Charles Darwin in 1842, Robert Plutchick in 1980, Paul Ekman in 1994 and many more since, the common thought in psychology is that we have core emotions and then we have nuances of those emotions. For example, anger is a core emotion, and frustration is a nuance of anger.

Here are more fun facts about emotions:

Fun Fact 1: Emotions are electrochemical signals that flow through us in an unending cycle. They are released into your brain and flow all throughout your body in response to your perceptions about the world.

Fun Fact 2: Emotions are neutral. There are no such thing as good or bad emotions, you just find some more comfortable than others.

Fun Fact 3: Emotions function to guide us to survive and thrive. They focus your attention and motivate you toward a specific course of action.

Fun Fact 4: Each emotion has a purpose:

- **Example 1: Anger** is a signal that your path is blocked. It focuses your attention on the threat and motivates a response of fighting or pushing through the obstacle. It can be used destructively, of course, but it also gives you the energy to find solutions to a pressing problem.

- **Example 2: Joy** focuses your attention on an opportunity and motivates you to do more of whatever you are doing. You feel joy when you experience meaning and connection, and the purpose of the emotion is to tell you that those are good things which you should seek out.

Fun Fact 5: Emotions are contagious. They spread very fast. You can 'catch' both positive and negative emotions, and it's part of your survival system as pack animals. This is why we have something called 'crowd mentality'.

Fun Fact 6: Emotions are different from feelings and moods. I had it explained to me as emotions are felt in an instance, they are an immediate response which lasts for seconds or minutes. When you mix emotions with thought, they can create a mood which can last for hours or days. Therefore, the core difference between the two is the period of time they last and to what extent your thoughts are involved.

Having an understanding of emotions helps you to manage emotions effectively which leads to healthy emotional wellness. This process requires your ability to access your wise mindset over your emotional and rational mindset.

The Wise Mindset

When I was learning to understand about emotions and first came across the concept of the wise mindset, it took me back to my friend Samantha's seventh birthday party when she fell off a seesaw and broke her arm because she was not holding on. Since then, I have turned this unfortunate incident into an analogy that I am going to share with you.

Imagine you have a seesaw with three children sat on it; the children are best friends and always play together.

- The **emotional** child is sat on one end, holding on to

the handles.

- The **rational** child is sat on the other end, also holding onto the handles.

- The **wise** child is sat firmly in the centre, with no handles to hold on to.

The aim is for all children to remain safe on the seesaw whilst playing together

All three children first start playing on the seesaw slowly and calmly, giggling away.

At first, as the emotional child moves up and then the rational child moves up, the wise child feels limited amounts of turbulence, moving only slightly as the two ends of the seesaw move up and down calmly.

But then the emotional child and the rational child start to build momentum, causing each end of the seesaw to swing higher and higher into the air. The turbulence is too much for the wise child, and they fall off the seesaw and are no longer able to play.

The learning point from this is that we all have three mindsets: emotional, rational and wise. Life is like that seesaw: it will produce different levels of turbulence throughout our lifetime. You can only manage it effectively if you use your wise mindset, which can only come in to play if your emotional mindset and rational mindset are balanced, because that is how wisdom and clarity of the mind are achieved.

From the analogy's perspective, your role in life is to keep the wise child safe – if you do this, you use the best of your emotional mindset and the best of your rational mindset for a balanced outcome and improved emotional wellness. You may have heard or seen a similar concept expressed in **emotional intelligence (EI).**

Emotional Intelligence

Emotional intelligence is the ability to understand and manifest your emotions positively, so you are able to empathise with others, develop effective communication skills, overcome challenges and conflict, and manage your stress levels.

Emotional intelligence impacts your life in a wide range of ways, from the relationships you build to the life goals you set yourself and through to how you not only connect with your feelings, but also how you use those feelings to make positive life decisions and take any necessary actions with confidence.

Your emotional intelligence commonly breaks into four core elements:

1. **Self-management** – how you manage your feelings and behaviours and adapt to life.

2. **Self-awareness** – understanding your emotions and how they affect your thoughts and behaviour.

3. **Social awareness** – your empathy towards others and your understanding of their thoughts, feelings and behaviours.

4. **Relationship management** – know how to develop and maintain good relationships.

The topic of emotional intelligence is gargantuan and deserves a book in its own right, so I am simply introducing it to you here. But what I want you to take away from this small introduction is that EI is an important tool for improving your wellness and wellbeing because it helps you to understand your emotions, so you are in a better position to control them, express them, and also understand them when they are being demonstrated by others. This provides you with the ability to navigate relationships, communications and interactions with others. Your emotional intelligence is the bridge between your internal world and external world (the world that exists within you and the world that exists externally of you) and it is a fundamental element needed in navigating both positively and effectively.

Example: A person with good EI demonstrates compassion and a good understanding of other people's emotional states. They are able to express themselves openly and respectfully because they understand their emotional state and can manage change well. They are good listeners and are not scared to be creative and think outside the box.

Resilience

Another core skill to develop in order to manage your emotions and improve your emotional wellness is resilience – the ability to cope with extreme stress-provoking events without experiencing any personal stress signs or symptoms. It is about having the ability to bounce back in the event of adversity, and it is about focusing on what you can control and learning to let go of what you can't. It requires you to learn to cope and adapt to inevitable challenges, problems and setbacks whilst managing the everyday challenges and stresses.

There are many models for resilience, but the one I find to be most helpful for my clients is Professor Derek Mowbray's model of Personal Resilience, which focuses on the three core areas of your personal control and the eight key elements within them:

1. **Personal control over self:** vision, self-confidence, organisation

2. **Personal control over responses to events:** problem-solving, interaction

3. **Personal control over responses to people:** relationships, self-awareness, determination.

The overall aim of resilience is to learn to focus on what you can control and to let go of everything you can't control. Resilience develops confidence and skills in the eight key elements which in turn helps you cope effectively with any given stressful situation.

To truly be able to improve your emotional wellness, not only will you need to develop the skills for balancing your emotions, but you will also need to make some changes to your internal world, the world that causes the emotional reactions to situations, your self-esteem and inner dialogue.

Example: A person who is resilient demonstrates optimism, and has an ability to get involved with arguments and discussions without becoming emotionally involved. They can respond well to criticism and are persistent when problem solving situations. They are able to make decisions effectively, do not let their time management suffer when they are under stress, and their mood is not easily affected by people.

Self-Esteem and Confidence

Self-esteem and confidence are two more terms that get confused a lot, so I want to clarify them both for you.

- **Confidence** is when you feel sure about yourself and your abilities to do something in a realistic and secure way rather than an arrogant way.

- **Self-esteem** is the opinion you have of yourself, your evaluation of your own worth and your value.

You can be a very confident person with low self-esteem, you can also be someone who lacks confidence but has good self-esteem, and you can lack both. The great news is you can also develop both too.

I work with a lot of executives, business owners and those regarded as highly successful people, and I would say that 90% of the clients who come to see me suffer with low self-esteem and mixed levels of confidence, which shows what we see on the outside is not necessarily what is actually happening on the inside. That's the power of the inner world – it's all ours, and if it is unhealthy with low self-esteem, then we start to see ourselves and our life in a much more critical way. We feel less able to face the challenges that life throws at us, and that negative mindset can have an extremely detrimental effect on our lives and specifically our mental health.

To understand how to develop good self-esteem, you need to start with understanding what causes low self-esteem – and for the majority, it all starts with childhood.

Nurturing a child is like building a house, it happens brick by brick and takes many people to do it; parents, siblings, extended family, friends, teachers and even the media all play their part in building that house and nurturing that child. Everyone's role is important within the life of that child, and they stay a part of the child's foundations and structure forever, with all memories and experiences linked to those people kept within the subconscious and unconscious mind.

I once had a client say that they did not think the adults in their past played a part in their self-esteem at all. The client was in their early forties and so I asked them, *'Can you recall a conversation you had with a teacher when you were at school?'* They told me about how when they were twelve years old, their Maths teacher had told them they thought they were not bright enough in Maths. That client had gone on to become a senior level accountant in a huge international company and was working with me to manage their work-life balance and manage stress more effectively. Their stress was being triggered by feeling that they always had to do more, always had to give more, and the fundamental drive for this was a feeling of inadequacy. They asked me if I thought that teacher had been an important factor in their life and self-esteem – so I asked, *'How many other conversations do you remember having as a twelve year old?'* The answer was zero. So the fact that they were able to recall that one specific conversation with ease indicates that it was a powerful one, and that specific teacher's voice had remained a part of my client's subconscious for over thirty years…even driving the direction of their life.

That's the power we as adults have in a child's life – everything we do or don't do, just like everything we say and don't say, plays a part in building that house. If any bricks are missing from that house due to a turbulent childhood or negative messages about that child, such as they are not kind, not good, not strong, not smart, then those messages stay, creating an empty space instead of a solid brick, leaving big gaping holes in the building.

Those gaping holes due to the missing bricks can lead to a negative self-concept, negative self-talk, unrealistic expectations of yourself, people-pleasing tendencies, a reluctance to say 'no' to others, trust issues and a natural tendency to see the negative in every situation.

From my experience of working with my clients, the common themes for those with low self-esteem are:

- trying to fill the void they feel from those missing bricks with external factors, such as needing to gain praise from others in their work and their home life, which leads to perfectionism

- a negative inner dialogue, a voice inside their head, always telling them no matter how positive an achievement is, they could have done better.

Your internal dialogue is simply your thoughts, the little voice in your head that acts as a running commentary to your life. Some don't pay a lot of attention to it, while others are tuned into its every word, manipulating its meaning to match their emotions. The role of your inner voice is to apply logic to the world you experience. With a negative inner dialogue, the logic is skewed as it's driven by emotion. Think back to the analogy of the three children on the see saw, the emotional child at one end, the rational child at the other and the wise child sat in the middle. To be at our best, we want to access our wise mindset (keep our wise child safe) which means balancing our emotional side with our rationale side. With regards to my original analogy, this means keeping the see saw stable.

I worked with another client who genuinely believed that every time they had an excellent annual appraisal and pay rise that the positive feedback was a lie and there must be an alternative motive for it. They simply could not accept that they were good at what they do, that they were good enough and that they deserved to be valued.

Low self-esteem can stop you living a fulfilling life simply by being a blocker between enjoying or engaging in things such as social situations, work events or learning new skills, because they make you feel unsafe. You may find yourself avoiding challenging and difficult situations in general and so develop an inability to cope with them when they do happen. And this way of living, these missing bricks in your wall caused in childhood, just reinforces those negative beliefs and self-concepts which can lead to mental health problems or self-defeating habits, such as drinking and drugs, as coping mechanisms for stress.

There is a process for developing your self-esteem and flipping the negative inner dialogue to a more positive and productive one, but you have to start with being really honest with yourself and accepting where that self-esteem might be today and where it came from. I always explain to my clients that the inner voice was once someone else's voice, someone else's words and you claimed them as your own, so now it's time to identify whose voice it was and give it back so you can hear your own voice again. That is the only way you can fill in the missing bricks of your self-esteem house and build your own inner home – it all happens internally, not externally.

Step one in the 8Wise process is to identify your current wellness level against each dimension and element, and I will talk you through the assessment process in later chapters. Please don't be scared if your emotional wellness is not where it needs to be right now – taking responsibility and becoming accountable for actively improving it can start immediately, and you can feel the benefits of improving your emotional wellness quite quickly too. So, embrace the change and the challenges ahead as they will lead to lifelong positive outcomes for your mind and your body.

> *If you want to jump ahead to the action phase for Emotional Wellness go to the following pages:*
>
> Assessment page: 227
> The Goal Setting Action Plan page: 207 & 285
> Activities, tools and tips page: 251

Physical Wellness

As a child, I was diagnosed with asthma, which basically meant school sports and exercise were unpleasant experiences for me, which is tragic because I was quite good at some of it at an early age. I also had inner ear issues and so was unable to swim for many of my school years, instead being forced to do extra study in the library with the other 'sick' kids *(I still love a library)*. To top it all off, I was allergic to a lot of things and had food intolerances coming out of my ears. This was the eighties, and I lived in a small town in Somerset, England. The only alternative to 'normal' food was to pay five times the price at the boutique health food shop, which my parents could not afford to do, so although we tried to implement a diet and exercise plan that worked for me and my 'uniqueness', we never really managed to embed something that stuck. As a result of this, I never developed a love for exercise or activity, and I had an unhealthy relationship with food from the age of eight. So, it is not surprising that I was prone to high levels of stress as both a child and adult and had my own mental health experiences, because I struggled to develop a solid foundation of wellness from a young age. As we know, mental health and physical health go hand in hand – they are not separate, and one affects the other. This is why in 8Wise, the second Foundation Dimension is your Physical Wellness because if you don't develop a good foundation of physical wellness, your mental and physical health will suffer – I can't even sugar coat that for you *(nutritional pun intended)*.

Fun Fact 1: Physical wellness promotes proper care of our bodies for optimal health and functioning.

Fun Fact 2: Positive physical health habits can help decrease your stress, lower your risk of a range of diseases and health problems (including stroke and heart disease), and increase your energy levels.

So, let's get physical, because whether we like it or not our physical health is crucial to our mental health, and so we must put a lot of effort in to developing and maintaining our physical wellness.

To do this requires you to take care of yourself through four focus areas: **Health, Sleep, Nutrition** and **Activity**. This will be of no surprise to you as the world is screaming at us daily to eat healthier, get more exercise, ensure you get adequate sleep and keep up-to-date with your medical check-ups (and that includes the dentist, smear tests and any other procedures that can be uncomfortable but life-saving).

Health

To be able to manage your health, you need to have a good understanding of your body so that you are able to identify when you feel it is not functioning effectively. It is difficult to do this if you do not have a healthy base level to work from. I don't need to tell you what is healthy and unhealthy for your body as it is constantly drummed into us, so you simply need to reduce the behaviours that increase your risk of disease and illness and increase the behaviours that reduce your risk of illness.

But we also have to be realistic – we can't prevent everything and so health issues will occur, and we need to be aware that those health issues can have an effect on your mental health too. For example, health related issues can make us feel anxious, or depressed, and being in pain can interfere with sleep, eating and mobility. Health related issues can also lead to low self-esteem, social isolation, stigma and discrimination. So, it is important to keep up with all regular health checks, implement an effective and realistic physical wellness self-care plan and to take care of your body as well as your mind. Most importantly – get support if or when you need it.

Sleep

One of the first questions I ask all my clients is 'How is your sleep?' If they say it's not so bad, I know we can tackle other issues and areas of wellness and wellbeing first, but if they say their sleep is poor or worse, then sleep is the place we start, because without quality sleep we cannot have a quality of life, no matter how much we might want to believe otherwise.

Having enough quality sleep is as essential to your survival as food and water. It is an important factor in a number of different brain functions, including how our nerve cells (neurons) communicate with each other, how we create memories, how we learn and how we concentrate. It even has the ability to remove toxins in your brain that build up while you are awake. Simply put – sleep is awesome, and I am talking as someone who experienced horrific episodes of insomnia.

Sleep affects almost every type of tissue and system in the body – from the brain, heart, and lungs to metabolism, immune function, mood, and disease resistance. Therefore, having sleep issues has quite a detrimental effect on your health and wellbeing.

From my personal and professional perspective, sleep is so very important, and you need to gain some deeper understanding of the sleep cycles and how much sleep is necessary for health and wellbeing.

Now, let's take a look at the different stages of sleep, also known as the sleep cycles. The first thing to understand is that there are two basic types of sleep that link to the brain activity listed above:

1. Rapid eye movement (REM) sleep

2. Non-REM sleep (which has three different stages).

The reason they are called cycles is because during quality sleep you cycle through all stages of non-REM and REM sleep several times in a typical night, with increasingly longer, deeper REM periods occurring towards morning.

Stage 1 non-REM sleep is the transition from being awake to sleep. This is a short period of relatively light sleep that only lasts a few minutes. During this period your heartbeat, breathing, and eye movements slow, and your muscles relax with occasional twitches. Your brain waves begin to slow from their daytime wakefulness patterns (Gamma to Beta, to Alpha and then to Theta and Delta, where sleep takes place).

Stage 2 non-REM sleep is the period where your brain waves are usually at Theta level; it's the light sleep before you enter deeper sleep, and during this stage your breathing and your heart beat slow, your muscles enter deep relaxation, your body temperature drops, and you stop having eye movement. Most of your repeated sleep cycles take place in this stage.

Stage 3 non-REM sleep is the period of deep sleep where your brain waves are in Delta, and the outcome of this stage is you will feel fully refreshed in the morning. It takes place mostly in the first half of your sleep. Your heartbeat and breathing are at their lowest, muscles are relaxed, and it may be difficult to awaken you.

REM sleep is where most of your dreaming happens. It is where you experience rapid eye movement due to your brain waves fluctuating towards being awake. Unlike with non-REM sleep, your heartbeat and blood pressure increase, and your breathing becomes irregular. Your arms and legs become temporarily paralyzed, preventing you from acting out your dreams. As you get older, you will spend less time in REM sleep.

Like most things in life, your overall sleep pattern will also change as you age. And, contrary to popular belief, there is no 'magic number' of hours sleep required that works for everyone within an age group; it really is dependent on the person, hence I always ask my clients to complete a sleep diary to identify their personal sleep pattern. And don't rely on sleep apps – they are not 100% accurate.

Research indicates that babies may need 16 to 18 hours per day, to boost growth and development. School-age children and teens may need approximately 9 to 10 hours of sleep, and most adults need 7 to 9 hours of sleep a night, which can transition into lighter interrupted sleep after the age of 60.

Also for those of you reading this thinking it is OK – 'I can catch up on my sleep on a weekend' – sorry to disappoint you, but research conducted by Harvard University states that there is no real way to recoup lost sleep. It's either achieved daily or not at all – literally meaning 'if you don't snooze, you lose.'

Diet

Four little letters that when put together create a word that can cause diverse emotions and opinions. I typed the word 'diet' into my browser, and it listed 1,140,000,000 results in less than a second, 0.57 seconds to be precise. That is how big a topic that little four-letter word is, and the confusion that comes with it is huge.

Now, I am not a nutritionist, so I am not going to go into great scientific detail on this subject; you have 1,140,000,000 other options for that. But I do want to try and clear up some of the confusion by clarifying some basic language:

Diet: This actually refers to the kinds of foods you habitually eat. So, when we say we are on a diet or need to manage our diet, it simply means we are actively making changes to our habitual food intake, for whatever positive results we are aiming to achieve.

Nutrition: This refers to the quality of the food you eat habitually, whether it is fresh or processed, rich in minerals and vitamins, its calorie density and how it is produced.

Balanced Diet: This refers to ensuring you eat a variety of foods so you can get the right nutritional balance to achieve and maintain a healthy body.

The aim of your habitual food intake is for it to be well balanced with all the foods that provide you with the necessary nutrition to keep you mentally and physically healthy. This is important because there is growing evidence to support the fact that nutrition may play a fundamental role in preventing, developing and managing diagnosed mental health problems such as depression, anxiety, schizophrenia, attention deficit hyperactivity disorder (ADHD) and dementia.

As already highlighted, there are literally millions of people providing information on 'diet' and 'diets' all across the internet and in every book store across the globe. There are many ways to ensure a balanced nutritious diet, but to reduce the risk of food affecting your brain function negatively, you need to reduce or limit two food groups from your diet.

1. Group one consists of those foods that create a temporary alteration in mood, such as caffeine and sugar.

2. Group two consists of foods that prevent the conversion of other foods into nutrients that the brain requires. Saturated fat is one example of this group.

What these two groups have in common is that most of the foods that contain them are highly processed, so my only recommendation for a healthy nutritious diet is to aim to reduce processed foods and increase natural whole foods for a healthy body and mind. I will leave it to the millions of nutrition specialists in the world to help you with the rest, but I will share some tools and techniques later that can help with this area.

Physical Activity

Let's just 'jump' right in with some clarity on this one with regards to what is classed as activity and what is classed as exercise, as this causes quite a bit of confusion for many of my clients.

Physical activity is any body movement that is carried out by your muscles and joints that requires more energy than when you are rested, for example walking, yoga or gardening.

Exercise is a type of physical activity, but it is a planned, structured, repetitive and intentional movement intended to improve or maintain physical fitness such as, for example, weight training, aerobics or sports.

Physical activity is essential for your wellness and wellbeing; in fact, the Centre for Disease Control states that if you are physically active for about 150 minutes a week, you have a 33% chance of reducing your risk of dying early from leading causes of death like heart disease and some cancers, and those benefits start to accumulate with any amount of moderate or vigorous-intensity physical activity.

So physical activity can help you live longer, which is great, but what's the point of living longer if your life is miserable because you have poor mental health? The good news is physical activity is good for your mental health too.

Physical activity releases chemicals in your brain called endorphins. These are chemicals produced by the body to relieve pain and emotional stress. They are created in the brain by our old friend the hypothalamus, along with the pituitary gland. They work in a similar way to what most countries call 'Class A' drugs, or 'opioids', which can produce feelings of euphoria. In the case of your mental health, along with that sense of euphoria, which is great for your overall wellbeing, they are also able to boost your self-esteem and increase your ability to concentrate too. Research suggests endorphin levels may be a factor in fibromyalgia, depression and other mental health issues, so physical activity is crucial for both your health and your wellbeing.

If you want to know how active you need to be for general health, here is some guidance for you.

- Adults aged 19-64 years – a minimum of 30 minutes of moderate intensity five times a week

- Young people aged 5-18 years – a minimum of 60 minutes of moderate or vigorous activity daily

- These minutes can be completed all at once or in smaller bite size chunks for convenience

- Moderate intensity means you will breathe heavier but won't be out of breath, and you will feel warm but not hot and sweaty

- Vigorous activity means your breathing will be much harder, making it difficult to talk; your heart rate will be rapid, and you will feel hot and sweaty

- You can start slowly and build up at a pace that suits you

- In general, high-intensity workouts produce more endorphins than moderate exercise does.

If you want to jump ahead to the action phase for Physical Wellness go to the following pages:

Assessment page: 229
The Goal Setting Action Plan page: 207 & 285
Activities, tools and tips page: 251

Summary:

Remember, step one in the 8Wise process is to identify your current wellness level against each dimension and element, and it doesn't matter where your current level is. Taking responsibility and becoming accountable for actively improving it will lead to lifelong positive outcomes for your mind and your body.

In a nutshell, the 8Wise Foundation Dimension of wellness focuses on developing a strong body and mind so you can then develop a secure structure for them. It is important to develop an awareness of both your emotional and physical wellness in order to identify your current wellness level against each – this then tells you where you need to start to improve your foundation dimensions, which will then help you to protect your longer-term mental and physical health.

I will share how you can do this in later chapters, but by the end of this book you will have the tools to assess yourself against the 8Wise Foundation Dimensions and implement an effective and realistic action plan for improving them for your overall health and wellbeing.

Chapter 7:

The Internal Dimensions

Now that we have looked at what gives you a solid foundation of wellness and wellbeing, we move internally to develop, identify, acknowledge and accept those more in-depth elements to who you are and what stimulates you in life. These next two elements, spiritual wellness and intellectual wellness, align very strongly to the foundation elements of emotional wellness and physical wellness because, generally speaking, the four of them combined are the bedrock of what is perceived as the holy trinity for achieving personal balance in yourself and in your life – Mind, Body and Soul.

The Foundation Dimension very much focuses on the mind and the body, and now we move onto the soul. As the previous chapter showed us, just like when we build a house and a home, we have to start with creating a solid foundation. In wellness and wellbeing this is the same, so your emotional wellness and physical wellness creates that solid foundation for you to build on. The rest of the build requires more energy, more detail, and so 8Wise moves you to the more in-depth areas of your world, starting with your inner world. In 8Wise we call the next stage of improving your wellness and wellbeing the Internal Dimension. Through this chapter I want to take you deeper into 'your' inner world so you can start to identify what really makes 'you' who 'you' are and why.

Spiritual Wellness

As always, first I need to bring some clarity to the party because in the dictionary 'spiritual' can mean two things:

1. relating to or affecting the human spirit or soul as opposed to material or physical things

2. relating to religion or religious belief.

If that is not confusing enough, other experts have their own definitions also:

- Christina Puchalski, MD, Director of the George Washington Institute for Spirituality and Health, states that 'spirituality is the aspect of humanity that refers to the way individuals seek and express meaning and purpose and the way they experience their connectedness to the moment, to self, to others, to nature, and to the significant or sacred.'

- Mario Beauregard and Denyse O'Leary, researchers and authors of *The Spiritual Brain* claim that 'spirituality means any experience that is thought to bring the experiencer into contact with the divine (in other words, not just any experience that feels meaningful).'

For me and 8Wise, spiritual wellness is a combination of all of them because spiritual wellness is achieved through having a sense of connection to something bigger than ourselves in order to understand ourselves. I believe that spiritual wellness can help us to understand the meaning in life and, more specifically, the meaning in our own life. It helps us to identify our purpose and accept who we are, warts and all, as an individual. I believe that through developing this level of self-acceptance and understanding, we can also develop strong self-esteem and a feeling of peace and inner calm, which can also help develop empathy towards others.

Spiritual wellness is a critical element for our overall wellness and wellbeing – after all if we don't know who we are as individuals, we will never know the *who, what, where, when and why* to anything in our lives, such as:

- Who am I?
- Who do I want to be?
- Why do I think like that?
- Why do I believe that?
- Why do I respond like that?
- Why does that mean so much to me?
- What do I want?
- What do I need?
- What do I want to learn?

But before we get into it, let's address the elephant in the room: religion. I do not focus on the religious perspective of spirituality in 8Wise, not because I do not agree with it, but because I respect that there are many perspectives on religion, and I do not want to undermine any of them. I respect a person's belief system even if it does not align with my own. I understand that many people do find their spiritual wellness through their specific religious practice, and I want to assure you that 8Wise does not try to move you away from that in any way. If anything, I simply want you to understand which elements of spiritual wellness have the most positive impact on your overall wellness and wellbeing, whether you perceive that as your religious practice or your spiritual practice – the key is you do it.

Let's start with something easy – why are we here? I am kidding of course, but by answering this very simple but important question (*eeek*) you can achieve spiritual wellness. **Spiritual wellness** is a personal matter involving values and beliefs. It leads us to strive for inner peace, harmony within ourselves and with others, whilst also balancing our inner needs with the needs of the wider world. It promotes self-honesty and awareness, and along with it comes a sense of self-confidence and self-awareness. If you are looking for better self-esteem, then you need to develop your spiritual wellness.

To develop effective spiritual wellness through 8Wise, you will focus on three key areas; beliefs, values and purpose, and how you manifest each of them into your daily life. To live an authentic life, you need to be truly honest with yourself. You need to understand yourself, accept yourself, be confident in that knowledge of who you are and why you are that way, so that you are able to express that in your everyday life. When the life you live aligns with the values, beliefs and purpose you have, you are at your strongest, mentally and physically – let me demonstrate this to you through the example of 'the mid-life crisis'.

Mid-life Crisis

I work with a lot of people between the ages of 30 and 55, and the issues that a person experiences during this period are often mis-labelled as a mid-life crisis. Now, I will be blunt with you – I do not believe in the notion of a mid-life crisis. Don't get me wrong, I 100% believe that someone can experience something that can feel like they are in crisis, but I think the term undermines the powerful experience a person is having during this stage in their life, because used rightly and labelled correctly it can be the most empowering experience of a person's life. Let me explain. I believe that from the time we are born we are told by our families, our cultures, and our society how to live. For example, in the western world, generally speaking, the path is: learn to walk and talk, go to school, get smart, get good grades, make friends, go to college or university, get a good job, meet someone, buy a house, get married, have kids and then raise kids effectively so they can continue the cycle. Once we have done this, we then continue to live a settled life until we retire, by which time we have earned the right to rest and enjoy our final years before we die.

What I find with my 'mid-life crisis' clients is that they have followed the rule book and have reached the stage that hasn't been as clearly laid out with clear goals for them by society – the *'continue to live a settled life'* stage. A blank canvass can be daunting, because when they are not striving for things, their daily lives are not cluttered with the same levels of exhaustion they may have been experiencing in past decades. And when that happens, a different voice appears in their heads – their own – and that brings what feels like a crisis, because it is unknown to them and they have not yet developed a trust in it, so they start to think .

They start to truly think with their own inner voice, thinking for themselves for the first time, rather than thinking with the inner voice society has forced them to listen to, and this all happens at a time when they start to become in tune with their own mortality.

When we are young, our mortality tends to be a distant thought in our minds; we almost feel the future is guaranteed, and so we walk up that huge mountain of goals society has laid out for us, experiencing success, failures and loss, thinking that when we get to the top the views will be amazing. For many, however, the truth is that if they are lucky enough to get to the top, half of their lives have gone, and the view is not what they hoped for.

As we move through the stages of life, we start to experience and observe the traumas life throws at us and at the people around us. We see sickness, death, broken hearts, broken friendships, lost careers and we start to question who we are, what we want and where our lives are going.

The common theme with my clients is that they start to develop their own wants and needs as they reconnect with their 'authentic self', meaning they want to realign with their true or real self, living their life according to their own values and goals, rather than those placed upon them by others or society in general. They start to question the life they have led, whether they are happy or satisfied, and if they are loved or appreciated. They start to think selfishly with regards to their own wants and needs and feel guilty when they act on them. This group of people feels confused because to others it seems so out of character, but to me, what I see is growth, the start of the journey that Maslow called his fifth tier on his Hierarchy of Needs – Self-Actualisation.

As we move through life on the road to self-actualisation, we develop our wisdom from our experiences and observations along with our values and beliefs. It starts to drive our minds, our thoughts, feelings and behaviours. This can bring us to a new crossroads in life that leads to a wide range of life transitions and feelings.

The *'continue to live a settled life'* stage is unchartered territory for us – there is no road map anymore; we are simply on an open road, heading towards retirement and then, in reality, death. That realisation may feel scary, daunting and overwhelming. It can lead to uncharacteristic behaviours, life changes, and feelings of anger, guilt, uncertainty, self-loathing and indecisiveness, which can lead to a feeling of overpowering chaos, which is why we call it a 'crisis'. A crisis is a 'a time of great disagreement, confusion, or suffering'.

This crossroads can lead to self-empowerment and achieving a life that truly fulfils you because it provides you with an opportunity for self-reflection and self-evaluation of your life to date. This is where its merges beautifully with spiritual wellness, because the core areas you need to reflect on are values, beliefs and purpose.

If you are reading this and thinking, 'I'm too young to be having a mid-life crisis but I am experiencing similar thoughts and levels of confusion,' for me, that just proves there is no such thing as a mid-life crisis and that we all start our journey towards self-actualisation at different stages in our life. Over recent years, we have seen the growing concept of a quarter-life crisis, which is a crisis involving anxiety over the direction and quality of one's life.

The concept of a quarter life crisis is most commonly experienced between the ages 25 and 35, when someone enters the 'real world' after leaving home, graduating or starting their first job. But again, from my perspective this period is not a crisis. It is simply the outcome of the self-reflection and decision-making process that comes with the 'rite of passage' from childhood to adulthood. But what I have learnt through my work as a psychotherapist is that we live in a world that is obsessed with labels, and so calling it a 'crisis' ticks the label box.

When we look at the term 'crisis' it actually means 'a situation in which something or someone is affected by one or more very serious problems'. Please note the words I have underlined. In my humble opinion, although it is no doubt daunting, uncomfortable and stressful to have to start making decisions about your life and be fully accountable for your life for the first time, it's not a crisis in the true sense of the word. It is a step towards self-actualisation, which is a powerful and positive process putting you in tune with who you are, helping you to align your life journey with your values, beliefs and purpose. So calling it a crisis because you perceive the process as a problem, a failing in your inability to cope with your life, or an opportunity to compare yourself to others (when the work you actually need to do is internal, not external) undermines the importance of the process and derails you from achieving self-actualisation.

Identifying this phase as a crisis simply leads to you accepting a negative label that can stick with you for a long time, manifesting into negative thoughts, feelings and beliefs about yourself which are, in fact, all false, but can lead to mental health issues, which can then lead to a genuine personal crisis. It becomes a self-fulfilling label, albeit one where the consequences can affect your overall wellness and wellbeing, and therefore your quality of life.

So, to clarify, the concepts of what are known as any form of 'life crisis' are part of your unique journey, which can't be compared to anyone else's because no one else has ever and will never experience your life the way you have. It is from this philosophy the concept of 'don't judge a man before you have walked a mile in his shoes' derives, because the truth is you will never walk in them, and so you should never judge him. No matter what stage in your life you are in, it is important to understand yourself through your beliefs, values, and purpose, and live a life that manifests them positively. You will then be on the journey to achieving spiritual wellness, and to do this, the first step is to understand what each of these spiritual areas are.

Beliefs

In the process of beliefs, values and purpose, we first develop a belief about something which then builds our own personal belief system. A belief is an idea you have that you hold to be true. It can be based upon certainties such as maths or probabilities such as science and also matters of faith, and they are heavily influenced by external forces such as culture, faith, education, experience and mentors.

A belief does not develop quickly – we take our time to welcome things into our belief system. As I have previously mentioned, we are intelligent creatures, and we have an inbuilt learning system that we use to determine whether we will accept a belief into our belief system or not. We need to process a belief at our own pace and so whilst we are doing this, the concept of that belief stays with us until we are ready to either accept it as truth and adopt it into our own belief system, or reject it. We evaluate the belief, and we search for evidence that the belief is true to us, and when we accept it as a truth, it then forms part of our belief system and we will defend it and act upon it. Our belief system can then drive our thoughts, feelings and actions.

We have two types of belief: self-belief and our belief regarding the world around us. Self-belief is at the core of what motivates us; it influences our goals and the directions we take to accomplish them. Our self-belief is so powerful that it can heavily influence all parts of our life, from the relationships we enter, the careers we want, to the lifestyle we choose to live. It can also influence what we choose not to pursue and accomplish in life too.

Our belief regarding the world around us relates to how we make sense of the world we exist in. This may come from education and teachings, it may come from cultural understanding, and it may come from personal experience. Wherever our belief regarding the world comes from, it shapes our interaction with it.

Our self-beliefs are our guiding principles; they are how we assess our personal capabilities and achievements, and if they are harnessed correctly, they are a powerful and positive source, helping us to accomplish great things. But if they are harnessed negatively, they will hold us back and can cause turbulence in our lives.

Overall, our self-belief determines what we do, how we do it, and how we view our accomplishments.

Three examples of core self-beliefs are:

1. **Control:** Our assessment of how much control we have over our lives and our destiny. We view this from either an external focus or an internal focus. If you have an external focus you may feel that you have no direct control over your life – life happens to you, so you always have something to blame. If you have an internal focus it triggers personal growth and development, so you take responsibility and accountability for your own success, failures and actions.

2. **Competency:** Our assessment of our overall ability to achieve desired outcomes and whether we feel we have the skills and abilities needed to achieve them. We tend to assess our capabilities based on the past,

present and future concepts. Past performance, present challenges and future anticipations and our conclusions tend to be based on presumption rather than facts or tangible evidence.

3. **Value:** The degree of value we associate with different task outcomes. For example, if you add low value to a potential goal or task, you may be more reluctant to invest effort, whereas if you add high value to an outcome, then the level of effort you are willing to invest will be increased. How you value a task will depend on the intrinsic value (how much you enjoy doing the task) and utility value (how useful you perceive the task). The value we place on something derives from the values that we have, and our beliefs influence our values.

Values

Values are our basic and fundamental beliefs – they define us, guide us and motivate our attitudes, our decisions and our actions. They are an extension of us and who we truly are at our core. They are what I call our 'authentic self' and are ultimately the key influencer in our identity. We can't hide from them because they are reflected in every way we choose to behave, every action we take and emotion we feel. And it is our values that trigger them.

When working on values with my own clients, many will state the values they 'wish' they had, covering up or being blind to the values they actually have. We can lie to ourselves about what our core values are; in fact, we can try and live a life aligning to the core values we wish we had rather than those we actually have, but this leads us to become disconnected from ourselves. We may do this because we are ashamed of the values we have, or it may be because we are in the process of developing a different set of values through personal growth and self-development, or we might simply be blind to our true core values. Either way, the disconnection creates disillusion either in who we are, the life we live, or the world around us. Through disillusion comes turbulence, confusion and chaos, which leaves us vulnerable to stress, and we know where stress can lead – sickness and unhappiness.

Many clients come to me claiming they 'feel lost' or they 'need to find themselves', and what this really means is that they feel disconnected from their values which are their core drivers. Their behaviours and actions are not aligned with their core values, and so they are disconnected from their authentic self, they don't know who they are, and they don't have a strong sense of identity. To develop a strong sense of identity, you need to identify your values and realign your behaviours to them; only then will you be able to live a life where you are truly your authentic self.

We develop our values from a range of sources: our parents, our family, our culture, our religion, society, and from our own life experiences. From all of these sources, we choose what we find important in our lives, what we want to prioritise, what we find of worth to us and what will help us achieve what we want. It is this process, this thinking, from which we make choices that come to define us. So, if we take someone who may believe themselves to be having a mid-life crisis for example, it may simply be that the life they lived was not aligned to their true values, or that those values have changed and they now need to start reclaiming their identify by redefining their values and living an authentic life aligned with them. To do this, they will need to follow three simple steps:

1. Identify their values.

2. Prioritise their values based on their goals and ideals.

3. Live by them.

> I will talk you through all three things in a later chapter, but for those of you who like a spoiler, go to pages 274-284

Now that you have an understanding of what lies at your core and drives you on a day-to-day basis, you need to understand how they influence your purpose.

Purpose

The only guarantees we have in life are that we will one day die, that life is not forever, and unless we are diagnosed with a terminal illness, the ending is not pre-determined and so we have no knowledge of the exact amount of time we have. If we were to live our lives by that knowledge, where would our motivation come from? As intellectual beings, and because we can't control those facts, we instead look for control elsewhere. What we focus on is the time we do have and what we can do with it. Goals, dreams and desires are what motivate us. They are heavily influenced by beliefs and values and they come together to give us our purpose – the reason why we do something or create something and the things that have great personal meaning to us.

I understand our purpose to be the answer to a great question I once read when I was sat on a beach in Mexico, 'What can I do with my time that is important?' What this question basically comes down to is: 'How can I influence the world positively in a way that has great meaning to myself whilst I am here?'

This purpose does not need to be something you decide upon as a child and stick with; instead, it will most likely change over time as you develop, accept and align with your identity, from childhood to adulthood. It is, of course, accessible at any age if you are willing to explore who you are as a person and act upon those findings. That's why 8Wise encourages you explore who you are, what you believe, what you value, what you live for and what you want to achieve. By doing this, you will develop a strong sense of your own identity, and through that, you can achieve Maslow's fifth level on his Hierarchy of Needs – Self-Actualisation, through self-acceptance and understanding. And that's the key to spiritual wellness in general. It's about taking the time, at any age, whenever you feel ready, to understand yourself and develop a strong sense of identity through your beliefs, core value and purpose, which reflect your life journey and the time you have whilst you are here.

It can't just stop with knowing them and understanding them though; you need to embed them so they can manifest into your actions, behaviours and daily practices. Spiritual wellness cannot be something you simply talk about; this is something where walking the walk really matters. You need to engage in actions, in tasks, in practices that reflect your spiritual wellness in order to maintain your spiritual wellness, because you will soon feel 'out of control', 'lost', 'demotivated' and 'disengaged' with life if you do not live internally and externally by your beliefs, values and purpose.

Then, and only then, have you really gained spiritual balance. So then, and only then, will you really find the inner peace that, along with your emotional and physical wellness, creates the bedrock of your overall wellness and wellbeing. Mind, body and soul equals emotional, physical and spiritual, the three graces for your wellness and wellbeing.

If you want to jump ahead to the action phase for Spiritual Wellness go to the following pages:

Assessment page: 231
The Goal Setting Action Plan page: 207 & 285
Activities, tools and tips page: 251

Intellectual Wellness

Without intelligence, the human species would not have survived, and it's what puts us at the top of the food chain. Our daily actions since birth require us to use our intelligence for problem solving to ensure survival as well as expressing ourselves effectively, to ensure we grow and evolve. As you may remember, this is my theory for the meaning of life. So, now you know how 8Wise influenced my beliefs and how my beliefs influenced 8Wise. My theory of 'a meaningful life' is to live a life of authentic purpose, which I believe is achieved through spiritual wellness. My theory for 'the meaning of life', is to survive and evolve, which I believe is achieved through intellectual wellness, hence the importance of these two 8Wise internal dimensions.

From the 8Wise perspective, when you have established who you are through the exploration of your spiritual wellness, you then need to move on to establishing what interests you and how to use your inbuilt intelligence systems to access that information for learning, development and personal growth – all of which leads to being more equipped for survival and evolving.

So, stop and have a quick think: Are you striving for personal growth? Do you allow yourself the sense of curiosity? Are you willing to seek out new information? Are you motivated to learn new skills? Are you able to use your intellect to make good decisions and think critically with an openness to new ideas? If so, you have developed intellectual wellness; if not – then you need to, because your mind is craving it.

Intellectual wellness is about knowing what interests you. It requires you to be willing to expand your skills, knowledge and creative abilities, and value creativity, curiosity, and lifelong learning. This can be achieved through a multitude of activities such as hobbies, reading, taking a course, learning a new language, playing an instrument etc. Basically, it can be anything that challenges you and takes you out of your comfort zone. Stepping out of your comfort zone will help you to develop your mental health, intellectual health and overall wellness.

Comfort Zone

Let's get straight to the clarity bit. A comfort zone is a psychological state in which things feel familiar to you and you are at ease and perceive that you are in control of your environment. In this space you experience low levels of anxiety and stress and a steady level of performance is possible. You may feel like life is plain sailing, when in reality it is anything but, because the fact is you are not sailing at all, you are simply stuck in the harbour.

Do you remember my earlier analogy of a ship sailing through life? Well, just like a ship was not designed to stay in the harbour, you are also not built to stay in the same comfortable place for all of your life either. You were born for challenge; you were born with the tools to navigate change. You were born with the intelligence to push boundaries in order to unlock your potential and achieve whatever brings you meaning and purpose in your life. You were built to sail the ocean and ride the waves of life.

When you first start to learn and develop knowledge, behaviours and skills, it's exciting, new and challenging, and at times it can be difficult, scary and stressful. Then it becomes easier, less challenging, less exciting and safe – it becomes comfortable.

Comfort is fine for a short period of time; it's easy to do what you're used to doing and stay within the confines of least resistance. But choosing to make comfort a space to exist in changes it from a healthy space to an unhealthy one, it becomes a prison that holds you back in life and the longer you stay in it, the bigger your fear grows about leaving it. Eventually, you will have to leave it, whether that be through choice or forced upon you by external factors moving you into a new direction. The truth is that if you want to make progress in your life, you need to break free from what holds you back, and that means escaping the self-inflicted prison that is your comfort zone – it means letting your ship leave the harbour and sail the seas.

Now, I appreciate this sounds scary, but you don't have to go full steam ahead – you can take it slow and simply move from your comfort zone through to the other zones as listed below:

- **Fear Zone:** Outside of your comfort zone, this is the first zone you need to get through. It is where you lack confidence and self-esteem. You can be affected by the thoughts and opinions of others and find excuses to step back into your comfort zone. If the fear zone is utilised correctly, you can access your 'optimal anxiety'. Optimal anxiety is the state of anxiety when your fight or flight response first triggers symptoms and arouses your senses for optimal performance. If you work through this zone, you move onto the next one.

- **Learning Zone:** This is the second zone you need to work through; it is where you learn new skills, deal with challenges and problems and extend your comfort zone. In this zone, you start to pursue your dreams, try new things, lead with courage, seek out opportunities and explore new things. Through learning and perseverance, you will finally reach the growth zone.

- **Growth Zone:** This is the third and final zone for you to work through. It is where you find your purpose, use your skills to help others and show empathy to yourself and others too. When you are in the growth zone, you are able to live in the present whilst adapting to change with a focus on the future. The growth zone is where you are able to practice calmness, patience, effective relationships and creativity. By remaining humble, persistent and mentally strong, you will be able to survive in this growth zone. You will eventually set new goals and achieve your major goals.

The key to moving out of your comfort zone towards your growth zone is to tap into your intelligence – and note this does not mean how clever you are or how smart you are. Everyone has intelligence – it just might get demonstrated in a way different to that which schools focus on. Sadly, our perception of our own intelligence tends to depend on how good we were at school which, to clarify, is not an effective marker for your intelligence as it is only 1/8 of the intelligence story, so don't write yourself off just yet.

Eight Types of Intelligence

In 1983, Harvard psychologist, Howard Gardner, developed a theory of multiple intelligences outlined in his book *Frames of Mind*, where he identified the existence of areas in the human brain that correspond to certain spaces of knowledge and intellectual competencies. This is one of the many theories on multiple intelligence, and it is the one that I find my clients respond best to, as it is a very simple demonstration that they don't have to be defined by how good they were at school. Your school experience does not have to define how smart, clever or intelligent you are, or more importantly, how intelligent you believe yourself to be. That thinking simply holds you back from trying and achieving new things, and it is inaccurate. So the key message of this theory of multiple intelligence is that although for many years it was argued there was only one form of intelligence type, known as the G Factor (generalised intelligence), more modern studies show that there are many more types of intelligence, meaning that we are smart, clever, boffins, geeks, intelligent in many different ways – you just need to identify and accept yours. Howard Gardner defined eight types of intelligence to help you do exactly that, but I would encourage you to read up on others:

1. Linguistic Intelligence *('word smart')*

If you have a sensitivity to the spoken and written language, an ability to learn languages, and a capacity to use language to accomplish certain goals then, just like William Shakespeare, you are linguistically intelligent.
Example: Writers, Lawyers, Speakers

2. Logical-Mathematical Intelligence *('number/reasoning smart')*

If you have the capacity to analyse problems logically, carry out mathematical operations, and investigate issues scientifically then, just like Bill Gates, you are logically-mathematically intelligent.
Example: Scientist, Accountant, IT

3. Spatial Intelligence *('picture smart')*

If you have the potential to recognise and manipulate the patterns of wide space *(oceans and the sky)* as well as the patterns of more confined areas *(human body, buildings and rooms)*, then just like Amelia Earhart and Neil Armstrong, you are spatially intelligent.
Example: Pilots, Architects and Interior Designers

4. Bodily-Kinaesthetic Intelligence *('body smart')*

If you have the potential of using one's whole body or parts of the body *(hand, mouth)* to solve problems

through mind-body union, perform skills or create products, then just like Michael Jordan, you are bodily-kinaesthetically intelligent.
Example: Atheletes, Builders, Dancers, Actors

5. Musical Intelligence *('music smart')*

If you have skills in performing, composing and have an ability to recognise and create musical pitch, rhythm, timbre, and tone then not only were you born to be a rock god like Freddie Mercury, you are also musically intelligent.
Example: Musician, Singer, DJ

6. Interpersonal Intelligence *('people smart')*

If you have the capacity to understand the intentions, motivations, and desires of other people, work effectively with others, recognising their moods, desires, motivations, and intentions then, alongside Mahatma Gandhi, you are interpersonally intelligent.
Examples: Psychologist, Teacher, PR

7. Intrapersonal Intelligence *('self-smart')*

If you have the capacity to understand yourself, your own desires, fears, and capacities – and to use such information effectively to recognise and understand your own moods, desires, motivations, and intentions to regulate your own life – then along with Aristotle, you are intraper-

sonally intelligent.
Example: Therapist, Entrepreneur, Clergy

8. Naturalist intelligence *('nature smart')*

If you have the expertise to identify and distinguish among different types of plants, animals, and weather formations that are found in the natural world, then just like Sir David Attenborough and Dame Jane Goodall, you are naturalistically intelligent.
Example: Gardener, Geologist, Astronomer

The 8Wise process recommends that you identify your intelligence type or combination of types, as it is possible to be more than one. Understanding your preferred way of learning will help you move out of your comfort zone towards your growth zone for intellectual wellness, but this can only truly happen if you are able to clarify one other self-belief.

Goal Orientation: The types of intelligence stated above give you some understanding of how we are all different. We are different in the way we learn and also different in what interests us. Alongside our life experiences, it is what interests us that leads us to develop the goals we set ourselves. Have you ever thought about why you choose to pursue the goals you engage in and aim for? For example, you may choose to read this book to gain knowledge and personal development to boost your ego and look good to others. Or you may choose to do it to develop a satisfying new skill or ability for yourself.

If it is to look good to others, then you are more concerned with what other people think than you are in actually achieving your goal, and this will not support you with developing intellectual wellness.

Those who want to master new skills are more attached to the outcome of the goal and so are more inclined to ask for support when needed. They are better at monitoring tasks and measuring progress and are more willing to try new or alternative ways to reach their desired outcomes. This approach supports intellectual wellness much more.

Through the 8Wise approach, you can develop your intellectual wellness by developing a better understanding of what is holding you back within your comfort zone. You will be introduced to new and exciting ways of growing your mind and freeing your creativity through accessing your intelligence type for personally satisfying growth. Effective intellectual wellness can improve your critical thinking skills, problem-solving skills, and your concentration as well as your memory, all of which leads to improved wellness and wellbeing.

If you want to jump ahead to the action phase for Intellectual Wellness go to the following pages:

Assessment page: 234
The Goal Setting Action Plan page: 207 & 285
Activities, tools and tips page: 251

Summary:

Remember, step one in the 8Wise process is to identify your current wellness level against each dimension and element and it doesn't matter where your current level is, because through taking responsibility and becoming accountable for actively improving it will lead to lifelong positive outcomes for your mind and your body

The 8Wise Internal Dimension of wellness focuses on developing a better understanding of who you are as a person and what interests and stimulates your mind. It is important to not only identify your beliefs, values and purpose but to live a life that reflects them for authenticity and growth. When you have established them you then use them as your drivers for setting and achieving any goals you choose.

Through actively challenging your comfort zone and learning new things to achieve those goals you will achieve a better balance between spiritual and intellectual wellness. But it doesn't stop there, because all dimensions and their elements are interconnected; like dominos, one effects the other. By following the 8Wise process for the Internal dimensions, you will also improve the emotional and physical elements of the Foundation dimension too.

With a better sense of self through beliefs, values and purpose, and successfully achieving goals, you will boost your confidence and self-esteem. In turn, this then decreases the negativity of your inner dialogue, reducing any symptoms of stress, anxiety and low self-esteem that may have been triggered by it. The overall result is a reduction or prevention of some physical symptoms connected to stress, anxiety and low self-esteem. This means that by improving your spiritual and intellectual wellness you can protect your longer-term mental and physical health, boosting your wellness and wellbeing.

Chapter 8:

The External Dimensions

We have now covered the first half of the 8Wise journey and the first two 8Wise dimensions:

1. Foundation dimension for emotional wellness and physical wellness *(mental and physical health)*

2. Internal dimension for spiritual wellness and intellectual wellness *(who you are and what you want)*.

When you have learned to understand who you are through your spiritual wellness, and what stimulates you and motivates you to develop through your intellectual wellness, you are ready to move onto the next big step.

We are now moving away from the comfort of your internal world, the place only you can access, that nobody else sees until it is exposed. Where your thoughts, emotions, needs, wants, fears, expectations, perceptions, motivations, drivers, self-belief and self-esteem are all private. We are moving you outside. It's time to feel the sun on your face and reconnect with the outside world – welcome to the External dimension.

We can't only focus on our inner world, because it's only one side of who we are, and so for full wellness and wellbeing we need to ensure our internal world manifests into a positive external world for us. This means using our internal world to create a positive external world for ourselves. What is the point of getting strong and healthy with a deeper understanding of who you are and what you want if you then do nothing with it? Plus, whether you like it or not, you have an external world which tends to be the trigger for your internal world, so it's important to learn to interact with it and, to a degree, manage it.

In philosophy, the external world is *the world consisting of all the objects and events which are experienceable or whose existence is accepted by the human mind, but which exist independently of the mind – Alfred North Whitehead 1910.* Let's start by making this statement make some sense.

Imagine your entire world is split in half by a large mirror. On one side, you have your internal world, the world where only 'you' exist, and on the other side is your external world, where everyone of your physical experiences exists. Unlike your internal world, your external world is physical; you can see it, feel it, touch it, smell it, taste it, and so your mind accepts its existence, leading you to interact with it. But remember, I said they are split by a large mirror, and that's because for these two worlds to coexist and work in harmony together, your external world needs to be reflective of your internal world, meaning your beliefs, values, purpose and attitude need to manifest into your actions and reactions in your external world. Who you are in your external world needs to mirror who you are in your internal world because when it doesn't, you will be out of balance and you will feel the effects of that mentally and physically.

For example, if you have ever experienced an agitated state of mind or a state of intense anger or hatred, it is because your internal world and external world are not balanced. Your experiences in your external world do not align to who you are in your internal world, and this causes conflict, turmoil, upset and discomfort, which can manifest into both mental and physical signs and symptoms of stress, anxiety and depression.

This is why through 8Wise we focus on your internal world first, so you are able to understand who you are in the inside world and gain the knowledge you need to know how to manifest 'you' effectively into the external world for a healthy and fulfilling life.

8Wise breaks your external world into two core elements: environmental wellness and social wellness. This concept means that when you know who you are from your spiritual wellness, you then need to learn what the right environment is for you to exist in positively, and then you need to identify who the right people might be to welcome into that environment and your external world. It's time to manifest those beliefs, values and purpose into actions.

Environmental Wellness

What comes into your mind with the phrase 'world environment'? For me, it is nature, our natural environment, green fields, blue skies, waterfalls, autumn leaves and the ocean with white sands and crashing waves. These also happen to be my favourite external spaces to spend time in – they calm me, inspire me, and make me feel alive. They also remind me of how small I am in the grand scheme of things and give me perspective when I can feel my mind heading into chaos. It is very easy to think about environmental issues when you think of the word 'environment', and although that is a factor, environmental wellness is not solely focused on environmental issues. Don't get me wrong, I do not want to underplay the importance of what is currently happening to the environment, and our planet clearly needs our support.

Without nature, there are no humans. It has provided us with everything we needed to survive for thousands of years, and because we are a part of it we are also highly sensitive to it too, hence we feel a connection to certain outdoor natural environments. It plays a crucial part in our survival and we play a crucial part in its survival. So, we should be making more effort to understand nature and our wider environment, so that we can do everything in our power to preserve this beautiful planet that we are lucky enough to call home. But environmental wellness for health and wellbeing requires you to look at both the bigger and the smaller picture, and so we will look at your natural environment and your personal environment to establish effective environmental wellness for you.

So, let's start right there, with you. Where you were born, where you grow up, where you live, where you work – all these things impact on your ability to live a long, happy and healthy life. In 8Wise, environmental wellness promotes your positive interaction with nature and your personal environment, inspiring you to live a lifestyle that is respectful of your surroundings with an understanding of its importance on your health and wellbeing. When you become environmentally aware, you understand how your daily habits affect your environment and how your environment affects your daily habits and behaviours. Whether you realise it or not, how you feel is significantly impacted by your environment, both your natural environment and personal environment.

Here is a little exercise to get you to start thinking about your preferred environments.

Simply complete each part in order and see what your outcome is.

Part one: Think about your favourite place.

- ○ *Where is it?*

- ○ *What is it?*

- ○ *How does it make you feel?*

- ○ *What do you love about it?*

- ○ *Why?*

Does your favourite place bring you feelings of security and safety? If you feel unsafe in your environment, or if your surroundings are in chaos, it's difficult to feel good, and when you don't feel good, your wellness perishes. The 8Wise approach to your environmental wellness is to identify the factors that might be affecting your environmental wellness, understand why they are having an impact, and then implement a plan of action to change them that will benefit your personal environment as well as your natural environment.

To do this, both your natural environment and personal environment need to ensure three things:

1. Safety and security

2. Physical comfort
3. Psychological comfort

Safety and Security

As Maslow explained in his Hierarchy of Needs, humans have a strong need for safety and security, and so we look for those attributes in our environment. As a species we soon learnt that we needed water, food and shelter, so we chose environments that met those needs. Our needs may have adapted slightly as the world changed, but our primitive needs remain the same and so we always seek out environments that make us feel safe and secure.

Physical Comfort

In psychology, physical comfort is the feeling of wellbeing brought about by internal and environmental conditions. These conditions can be achieved through recreating experiences that are linked to pleasant memories that bring with them feelings of contentment and satisfaction, like nostalgia. An example of this is having some chicken soup when you feel ill whilst snuggling under your favourite blanket, because that's what made you feel better as a child. (Fun fact: food can play the same part, hence the name 'comfort food', but that is a whole other book.)

Psychological Comfort

Psychological comfort is all about being at peace with yourself. It is a state of calmness, being absent of anxiety, at a particular moment in time within a particular space and environment. When you achieve psychological comfort, you become more attentive and present in that moment, which is positive for health and wellbeing. It is why psychological comfort plays a big part in the workplace for performance reasons and also in healthcare to aid recovery. We feel psychological comfort when we feel unthreatened by an environment, and when we understand what makes us feel like that, we can then take that learning and implement it into any environment we choose, such as our workplace or our holiday destinations.

These three elements have been exploited for years by the commercial world in sectors such retail and hospitality to make you trust a brand and spend more money in their stores. Have you ever noticed how you go to a shop or supermarket for candles yet leave with a trolley full of items? Is that a coincidence? Is that possibly psychological manipulation? Is it psychological influence? Or is that just me?

Let's have a quick look at the concept known as shopper psychology; the psychology used to determine what people buy and how much they buy.

It was developed out of behavioural science studies, where the focus was on the ways that external factors such as the environment, colours and smells can influence a consumer's purchasing choices. A multi-sensory experience dramatically increases purchase behaviour. Have you ever wondered why in the supermarket the most popular products such as bread and eggs tend to be the furthest away? It is so you are forced to walk through the multi-sensory experience the store has set out for you throughout all of the different aisles, increasing your chances of buying other items, and it works, or at least it definitely does for me, I rarely walk out of a store buying only what I went in for, it's a running joke in my household. I am definitely influenced by the multi-sensory experience they set out for me – are you?

Developing Environmental Wellness

So, how do we develop environmental wellness? To start with, you need to be able to identify your environmental preferences, and to do this, you need to think about eight key principles:

Preferences	Examples
1. Preferred environment to be close to	the countryside, the city, the coast
2. Preferred climate	hot, cold, seasonal
3. Preferred location	country, county, town, city, village, hamlet, secluded
4. Preferred shelter	house, apartment, vehicle, dwelling
5. Preferred factors	culture, opportunities, recreation
6. Preferred external surroundings	noisy, silent, amenities
7. Preferred internal surroundings	cosy, minimalist, organised, colourful, bright
8. Preferred space	lounge, bedroom, kitchen, study, garden, garage

When we are able to identify our preferences, we are then able to use them to determine the important environments in our life:

Region: Your region is where you settle and should include the factors you have identified as important to you such as culture, climate and recreational provision.

Community: Because we are pack animals, one of the key parts of your environment is the community right around you, so you should make sure your environment provides you with an opportunity to build strong connections with those in your communities.

Home: As we have already established in earlier chapters, home is very important to your wellness and wellbeing. It is therefore important to ensure you have safe and stable housing within a living situation that is comfortable for you. This environment takes into consideration your preferences but is also affordable to live in, maintain and carry out home improvements if needed.

Workspace (School or work): You will spend so much time in your workspace during your lifetime it is important to ensure it is fit for purpose and brings out the best in you. Along with your preferences, it should work with your personality, be comfortable, secure and ergonomic with a healthy atmosphere (we will cover this more in later chapters).

Physical environment: We have a strong connection to the natural environment, so do you have access to it and does your physical environment allow you to interact and contribute to the natural environment in an environmentally friendly way that is sustainable with little to no contamination or pollution?

The key to environmental wellness is to never underestimate its importance because it includes the 'big stuff', such as nature, climate, location and home, but also the 'small stuff' such as material surroundings, valued objects and possessions.

Not only are you a product of your environment, but you also impact your environment, so environmental wellness requires you to acknowledge, respect and protect the natural environment as well as understand yourself well enough to create a positive, safe and secure personal environment. With core themes, preferences and needs you can then implement a healthy environment throughout your external world.

On a personal level, I know first-hand how important environment is on your overall health and wellbeing. As a child, I grew up in the beautiful Somerset countryside, which was stunning. I had access to the beach, forests, woodlands and wheat fields – it was idyllic. But I suffered with my mental health and the environment was one of the factors, because although I was surrounded by natural beauty (which is still an important environmental factor for me today) it was small, and by that I mean the town I grew up in was small. The people are wonderful and still are to this day but being surrounded by such a small community made me feel vulnerable, exposed and trapped.

To others I was shy but really I just felt unsafe, so I chose my own company, my inner world, over the external world, which led to isolation and mental health issues.

I finally moved away, to Liverpool, and the sense of freedom I had changed me. My confidence grew, and my self-esteem grew. I felt content enough to try bigger and better, so I went to Melbourne and then London, and I was so confident I even tried living in a village outside of London too, feeling safe in the knowledge that my day-to-day was still the 'hustle bustle' of London, and none of these environments effected my mental health negatively. But when I moved back to a different idyllic small town, those old feelings came up again and on top of some other factors, it led to a very dark period in my life. Fortunately, an opportunity came to move back to the place I call home and the city that had welcomed me with open arms and gave me the freedom to be myself all those years ago – Liverpool. Once again, it helped heal me, it helped me grow, it allowed me to be me, no longer invisible, and so I don't hide from my external world anymore – now I embrace it. I recommend you do too, which is why I feel it is such an important element to the 8Wise process. So take some time to review your external world and the environments you exist in. Are they healthy for you, mentally and physically? Do they bring out the best in you? Are you spending adequate time in the environments that bring out the best in you? Do you know your preferred environment? These questions alongside some of the tools that are in the next section can help you to improve your environmental wellness and make necessary changes if or where they may be needed.

If you want to jump ahead to the action phase for Environmental Wellness go to the following pages:

Assessment page: 237
The Goal Setting Action Plan page: 207 & 285
Activities, tools and tips page: 251

Social Wellness

Your environmental wellness can be highly influenced by the people you share your life with and the interactions that take place in it. It becomes closely linked to your social wellness, which focuses more on who you share your life with, the interactions you have, and their effect on you and your overall wellness. Alongside these factors, 8Wise also takes into consideration how you differentiate between healthy connections and toxic relations with the aim of building the healthy ones and letting go of the toxic ones.

Our relationships can offer support to us during difficult times, but they can also be the source of those difficult times. As humans we are pack animals (even the introverts – and I will come to that shortly), and we still enjoy spending time with others and in many cases need to for our health and wellbeing. As a psychotherapist, it is one of the first questions I ask a client, 'What support system do you have?' and if the answer is 'none', it becomes a priority in the therapeutic process to develop one. It is important to have a good understanding of which social system you have that supports you and provides you with a sense of connection and belonging, because when you have developed this understanding and actively spend adequate time within your social systems, you have then developed effective social wellness.

Social wellness involves building healthy, nurturing and supportive relationships, as well as fostering genuine connections with those around you. It also includes the ability to balance those relationships, such as the unique needs of your romantic relationships, with other social systems such as friends, family and colleagues, as they all play a crucial role in your life.

When developing 8Wise, my intention was always for it to help you develop and maintain a social system and support network with healthy boundaries, good use of honest communication skills and with no passive aggression. Therefore, there is a focus on you developing the confidence to be your authentic self and encouraging respectful interactions between you and your social systems that stimulate you *(intellectual wellness)*, that make you feel safe *(environmental wellness)*, that encourage you to try new activities that promote health and wellbeing *(emotional and physical wellness)* and lead to a more fulfilling life.

The journey of social wellness for me starts with your personality.

Personality Type

The concept of personality types and personality traits have played a part in both psychology and philosophy for a long time, dating as far back as Hippocrates (460 - 370 BC). To understand it and how it affects our wellness and wellbeing, let's first look at what personality actually means, and I refer to Salvatore Maddi for a strong definition.

> *Personality is a stable set of characteristics and tendencies that determine those commonalities and differences in the psychological behaviour*

(thoughts, feelings and actions) of people that have continuity in time and that may not be easily understood as the sole result of the social and biological pressure of the moment.

– Salvatore R. Maddi, *Personality Theories: A Comparative Analysis*

Although complicated, this wonderful description basically explains that our personality is built from our inner world and is projected into the external world through our behaviours. The factors from our inner world that build our personality are:

- our ego – our natural self, who we really are at our core

- attitude and beliefs – our nurtured self, from what we have learnt to develop our deep-rooted mental attitudes and beliefs

- values – how we manifest our attitudes and beliefs into what we say and do

- competencies – our knowledge and skills and what we have become good at doing

- behaviour – how we act or conduct ourselves, especially towards others.

Each of those listed are separate to each other and have their own identity, as well as being part of the personality. But these five factors create the different levels of your personality which, along with external factors such as climate, content, situation and environment, are how you navigate through your life.

In psychology, there are two core theories linked to personality: traits and types.

- **Personality traits** refers to the habitual patterns of behaviour, thought and emotions we have. It is a quantitative approach to understanding aspects of your personality that differ from person to person but are relatively consistent in all situations and influence your behaviour.

- **Personality type** refers to the psychological classification of different types of individuals. It is a qualitative approach to understanding the differences between people. With effective personality typologies you are able to increase your knowledge and understanding of yourself and others (which is the complete opposite of stereotyping). This approach enables you to predict relevant information about yourself and others which can support with life and situational strategy.

Although they are two different approaches, they can both be used to help us understand ourselves more, and most importantly for social wellness, understand others better too, so that you can build strong social systems and effective relationships.

Based on this, I use personality a lot in my private practice and also in my training. When it comes to personality, I am a 'fan girl' of psychoanalyst Carl Jung's groundbreaking theory of

Psychological Type (1921). According to Carl Jung, we are all predisposed to be dominant in either Extroversion or Introversion, which is about where we direct our energy, either outward towards the external world, or inward towards our internal world.

Extroversion is typically characterised by outgoingness, high energy, and/or talkativeness. In general, the term refers to a state of being where someone 'recharges,' or draws energy, from being with other people. Combined with one of the four cognitive functions (listed below), those with extrovert personality types navigate their life through their perception and understanding of the external world.

Introversion is typically characterised by someone being shy and reserved, who becomes exhausted by social engagements and interactions with too many people. People who are introverted tend to be inward turning, or focused more on internal thoughts, feelings and moods rather than seeking out external stimulation, and so navigate the world through their internal world.

Carl Jung claimed that whether our dominant type is Extroversion (E) or Introversion(I), it influences everything, including our cognitive functions which he called 'functional types': *Thinking (T), Feeling (F), Sensing (S) and Intuiting (N) (refer back to chapter two for more detailed explanation).*

From this theory, he created eight core personality types that are a combination of these functional types:

Extroverted Thinking (ET): An ET relies on logic and evidence to make all decisions and they use this formula to navigate through life as if this formula is a universal law. They often therefore struggle with anyone who does not follow it.

Introverted Thinking (IT): An IT, like an ET, is very logical; they need to know how things work at the deepest level and so are very analytical. They build complex models and systems in their minds to explain how things work and map any new information against their models, whilst willingly adapting their model if they feel new information is superior.

Extroverted Feeling (EF): An EF uses their cultural values and values relating to humankind to make decisions based on what is best for the greater good and the people. Relationships and connecting with people are important to an EF and they can find themselves planning their life around it, striving for harmony and organisation within groups.

Introverted Feeling (IF): An IF is one of the hardest cognitive functions to understand, explain and observe because everything takes place in their internal world. The only time you are able to see it is when they are behaving emotionally or selfishly. They make their decisions based on emotions and not facts and are incredibly sensitive. They are also incredibly empathetic and supportive of other humans, especially those in need.

Extroverted Sensing (ES): An ES likes to live in the present and not dwell on the past or overthink the future and is extremely observant. Highly influenced by their senses they can identify any change in an environment, and they like to live life at an 'on the go' pace which can leave them vulnerable to burnout.

Introverted Sensing (IS): An IS is very similar to an ES in that the senses play a dominant role in navigating life, but they tend to be linked to memory and previous stored experiences. So, they are able to experience something in 'real time', but quickly compare it to stored memory and experience.

Extroverted Intuition (EN): ENs are very visual and their intuitions often manifest in the form of symbols, images, dreams, and patterns. They are driven by inspiration and can be incredibly abstract in conversation. ENs are independent with an individualistic approach to life, they look for the meaning behind things and navigate through life by trying understanding the 'why's' to everything.

Introverted Intuition (IN): INs focus inwards, on the internal world of thoughts, ideas, and concepts to focus on the future. They rely heavily on gut feelings to navigate the world and trust the unconscious world, which makes it difficult for them to explain their thoughts and strategies. So, at times, they can be perceived as 'rambling'.

For me and the work I do, I have found that having a basic understanding of your own personality helps you to start reflecting on who you are and how you interact with the world. It also starts to introduce you to the concept of cognitive differences between people, and this can lead to the one simple understanding that everyone is different. Everyone's behaviour is linked to their own perception of their external and internal world, and so as soon as you can accept that and start to identify and respect those difference in others, you can start to be more prepared in all social systems. When it comes to social wellness, what really matters is who you have in your life.

Social wellbeing is hugely important to our overall wellbeing. It's also very complicated as it has a strong overlap to the other dimensions because all our social interactions are a result of our emotional, intellectual and spiritual elements. Our social wellness is hugely influenced by what kind of people we have in our lives and the cultural contexts we live in, so we need to focus on developing healthy and supportive relationships in what I have identified as the five core social systems.

Social Systems

Social system is a term used in sociology or social science (the study of society) to explain a complex arrangement of elements, including individuals, their values and their beliefs, as they relate to a whole. The whole can mean the country the social system exists in, or any the group. So, in simple terms, it means the structure made up of people that exists within something else such as a country, an organisation, a peer group or a team sport etc. Within 8Wise, we focus on five core social systems: primary, family, friends, colleagues and community.

Primary: This could also be understood as your intimate partner or your platonic companion, and for most people it is the one social system we strive to have and maintain. It is the one social system that life and social norms make us focus on. Because of the focus and importance we place on these primary relationships it can be devasting for us when these are unsuccessful. Or from an 8Wise point of view, when it is an unhealthy social system. To ensure social wellness within this social system, you need to make sure your partner of choice is positive about your interests, respects you and your boundaries, and who is someone you are able to communicate and problem solve with. To ensure social wellness, this relationship needs to bring out the strengths and skills in both people, as well as be safe and healthy.

For some simple self-reflection on your primary relationship, ask yourself, *Is the relationship mutually safe and supportive?*

Family: They are either with us from the moment we are born, or we find them later in life. They do not have to blood relatives, but either way they have the biggest impact on our lives, whether they stay in our lives or not. They can be a supportive system or a breeding ground for toxic relationships. What you need to be aware of is that mutually supportive relationships are important to your wellbeing, and it is very easy in a family social system to be taken for granted, or for expectations to be born out of family loyalty. But, for your social wellness you need to remove or at least reduce toxic relationships, even if it is a family member, and you are within your right to remove yourself from any abusive relationships. Don't get me wrong, the majority of family relationships are worth building, developing, fixing and keeping healthy, but don't accept a toxic relationship just because it falls under the umbrella of family – try to work through it or distance yourself from it for your social wellness.

Be honest with yourself, and ask the question, *How much support for each other is there within your family members?*

Friends: They are the close connections you make with people who are not your family, and they should add great quality to your life and life experiences; absence of friends can leave us feeling very lonely. Because friends are voluntarily in your life, we deem them precious and we can be incredibly protective of them, which means we can be very hurt when they present issues, and it can be incredibly difficult to let them go.

One of the strongest emotions we experience connected to relationships is loneliness or the fear of being companionless and alone. This fear can make us feel desperate to stay in the primary social system and a friends social system no matter how toxic it might become. Within a friendship, it can lead to the relationship and the support within the relationship becoming very one sided.

When it comes to a healthy friendship social system, ask yourself, *Can I be my true self in this relationship and how supported do I feel in my friendships?*

Colleagues: The truth is, if we work in an environment surrounded by colleagues then we will spend more time in our lives with those colleagues than with family and friends, through both work and/or school. In my own experience, these colleagues can become known as your 'work family' and can have a big impact on our day to day lives. On the flip side of this, it can feel very isolating when experiencing a colleague-free work environment.

For social wellness and wellbeing, we need to ensure these relationships are healthy with boundaries and support. We will cover more about the workplace in 'Occupational Wellness', but issues with colleagues can play havoc on our stress levels because we can't escape them as easily as other relationships in our lives, basically because we are contracted to spend time and share space with them. When a work relationship is unhealthy, it can impact every element of your life, but on the other hand, when a work relationship is healthy it can be one of the strongest support systems, and so it is worth working on.

To reflect on these relationships, ask yourself, *Is there a healthy balance in your work relationships? And do you trust them?*

Community: As we discussed earlier, we are pack animals, and so we seek to become one of the pack, whether that be family, friends or community. Communities play a vital role in our life as they link us to the external world of others. They provide us with a lot of experience and learning and improve our emotional wellness, our environmental wellness and our social wellness too. They can be your town, your school, your club, your team. We all vary on how connected we feel to the community and how much involvement we want to have with them, and so it is important to understand if you feel satisfied by your community interaction, and if not, then change it.

Ask yourself this: *Do you feel like you contribute to your community, and would you feel better if you were more involved, or maybe less involved with it?*

The key to having successful relationships is based on how you get along with each other. You have to be able to be assertive when it's needed and communicate openly with confidence and clarity. You need to be able to handle conflict using your understanding and knowledge of different personality types and people's different perspective on life due to their own internal and external worlds. You have to accept there are no inferior or superior people, just different behaviours, thoughts, ideas, emotions, experiences and labels. You need to accept that the only control you have over people is the control you have over yourself. No one has to do, think, feel or behave the way you think they should, and so you need to work through the frustrations and wider range of emotions that may come as a result of that.

In fact if there is one key learning I would like you to take away from reading this book it is this:

> For your own social wellness, try not to take things personally because what others say and do is a projection of their own reality formed by both their internal and external world and their unique experiences. Their perception of the world is not, and never will be, the same as yours.
>
> When you can become immune from internalising the opinions and actions of others, you will be able to prevent yourself from experiencing endless suffering, as well as being able to develop good self-esteem and self-belief.

I have said it before, and it is worth repeating: the negative thoughts and dialogue in your head might sound like your voice, but it once belonged to someone else. You internalised it and have accepted it as your own. Through accepting the opinions of others as simply that – their opinions and not necessarily your truth – the only voice you will hear in your mind is yours, and it will be authentic and true to who you are at your core. That is a much more effective guide for navigating through and living a fulfilling life.

If you want to jump ahead to the action phase for Social Wellness go to the following pages:

Assessment page: 240
The Goal Setting Action Plan page: 207 & 285
Activities, tools and tips page: 251

Summary:

The external world is where you physically interact, and it can be a danger zone because it collides with the external world of others too. But this can't be a reason to distance yourself from it or retract into your inner world. For overall wellness and wellbeing, your internal world and external world must be balanced, and you must interact with both of them effectively for that balance.

The 8Wise tools and techniques will help you to develop the knowledge and skills needed for you to establish and maintain this balance for a better quality of life and also for better health and wellbeing. It's about taking what you learnt about yourself in the internal dimension and putting it into positive actions in the external dimension. Through doing this, you live a life of authenticity and that makes the final dimension easier to navigate because from the external dimension we move to the lifestyle dimension, where you use everything you have learnt so far.

How do you use your knowledge and understanding from your emotional, physical, spiritual, intellectual, environmental and social wellness to develop the fulfilling lifestyle you want? The lifestyle that will bring you happiness and encourages good health and wellbeing and purpose?

It's time to create the life that you want the 8Wise way.

Chapter 9:

The Lifestyle Dimensions

Hopefully by now you are starting to understand the different elements that make up your wellness. You may find that it is forcing you to think about situations in your own life a little differently and also question things a little differently too. You may find that you are starting to have a better understanding as to why you may react to things in a certain way and you may find that overall you are starting to know yourself a little better. That's the power of the Foundation, Internal and External dimensions of your wellness, the elements that make up those dimensions within 8Wise and give you the knowledge that will help you evolve. This will help you survive challenging life transitions and experiences, which therefore improves your wellness and wellbeing ... but it doesn't stop there.

After building a strong foundation through emotional and physical wellness, you are able to manage your health and wellbeing better and put yourself in a stronger position to tackle the next layer.

The spiritual and intellectual wellness elements found in the Internal dimension ensure you understand yourself well enough to truly know who you are so you can accept yourself.

This enables you to live an authentic life with good self-esteem. Which, alongside understanding what stimulates you and triggers your desire for development and growth, through your intellectual wellness, creates a healthy and positive inner world for you.

When your inner world is strong, you are then able to tackle the external world with confidence, developing healthy environments to engage with and exist in for your environmental wellness. When you have this in place, you are then in a stronger position to welcome others into your external world and environment. You begin developing a good supportive social system through your social wellness and your external world becomes stronger and more aligned with your inner world, which ultimately makes you mentally stronger.

So, through these six elements so far, 8Wise has helped you to develop your:

- Health
- Happiness
- Self-acceptance and self-esteem
- Personal growth and lifelong learning
- Healthy and sustainable environments
- Supportive relationships.

Now, 8Wise wants to move you onto the final piece of the puzzle – the dimension that focuses on you nurturing and developing a fulfilling life from all of the new knowledge and understanding you have gained through the 8Wise dimensions so far.

Welcome to the Lifestyle Dimension.

The lifestyle dimension focuses on the two elements that help you to create the lifestyle you want and that will lead you to a fulfilling life. All of the other elements also play a part in this, but these final two elements are where most of your daily stress comes from. They are the elements you engage in so that you can build a life, develop a future, take care of your loved ones, build your home, engage with your environment and society, develop strong relationships, and ultimately create the lifestyle you want. And by aligning with your internal and external worlds your foundation dimension also remain strong.

The elements that make up the lifestyle dimension are occupational wellness and financial wellness. When we know who we are and what we want, we understand the life we want to live and what it takes to live it. This determines our lifestyle choice and the necessary means to achieving and maintaining it.

Occupational Wellness

This element focuses on your vocational responsibilities and they should never be underestimated when it comes to your overall wellness and wellbeing.

Have you ever wondered what the expected number of days and hours are for a work life? Now, I have said before I am not a numbers person, but I think this next section requires numbers, so let's do the maths:

- The average person works 222 days per year – 365 minus weekend and holidays.

- If they were to do that for 30 years, their work life days would be 6,660. Equation used: 222 x 30

- This of course would increase if people worked for 40 or 50 years to between 8,880 and 11,100 work life days.

What does that look like in hours?
If the average working day is 8 hours long then:

- For 30 years – 53,280 working hours in a lifetime

- For 40 years – 71,040 working hours in a lifetime

- For 50 years – 88,800 working hours in a lifetime

The average person will also commute approximately one hour per day for work too, which changes the daily hours to 9 and the lifetime numbers to:

- For 30 years – 59,940 working hours in a lifetime

- For 40 years – 79,920 working hours in a lifetime

- For 50 years – 99,900 working hours in a lifetime

That is, on average, nearly 80,000 hours within a lifetime that you could be spending away from your family, your friends, your interests and hobbies, to dedicate to work. This basic equation does not even take into consideration overtime and any additional hours you may work.

This is only your work life. The other two thirds of your life contain your childhood and your school years which are preparing you for the world of work so you can support the economy and your communities. Your retirement years are your earned rest time from your working life. Writer Annie Dillard famously said, 'How we spend our days is, of course, how we spend our lives.' (*The Writing Life, 1999*)

With so many days of our life spent in work, how you choose to work is how you choose to spend your life, which leads us into occupational wellness, because if you are going to spend so much time within the workplace you need to ensure that it contributes positively to your overall wellness and wellbeing and aligns to your internal and external dimensions of wellness too.

Think about your job and workplace for a minute.

- Do you enjoy going to work most days?

- Do you have a manageable workload at work?

- Do you feel that you can talk to your boss and co-workers when problems arise?

If you are able to answer yes to these questions then you already have good occupational wellness, but if you don't, you may want to investigate making some improvements.

Occupational wellness focuses on having a good work-life balance, building relationships with colleagues and effectively managing stress within the workplace. Therefore, occupational wellness is important because, as we have already identified, we spend so much time at work, we need to enjoy what we do. When we are able to do that, we then have a deeper sense of meaning and purpose in our lives, which promotes positive wellness and wellbeing.

One way to accomplish this goal is by finding work that is not only financially rewarding but also meaningful to you too. When you find work that fits your skills, interests, and values, this can better support and maintain your goals for occupational wellness.

8Wise supports you to develop a clear vision for your career goals and set action plans on how to achieve them. Through the tools and tips, you will find in later chapters, it also supports you to develop the stress management techniques that enable you to secure an effective work-life balance, so that those 80,000 plus hours don't affect the other areas of your life or your health negatively.

I have suffered with my occupational wellness in the past and so I have a personal and professional understanding of how important it is to your wellness and wellbeing. And because you will spend more time at work with your colleagues throughout your life than you probably will with your family and friends, it is crucial that you learn to develop good occupational wellness so that it does not filter across and cause you too many issues in the other dimensions too.

Developing occupational wellness requires you to follow two steps:

1. Be able to identify the positive signs of occupational wellness

2. Be able to implement strategies for improving occupational wellness

The signs of occupational wellness include:

- having the opportunity to regularly engage in motivating, stimulating and interesting work that supports you in using your skills, expertise and knowledge

- having an understanding of how to balance your work with healthy and beneficial leisure time

- having an opportunity to work in ways that suit your personality and personal learning style

- regularly experiencing effective communication with others whilst having the opportunity to work either in collaboration with colleagues or independently

- being inspired and challenged at work and continuously learning and developing within your role or your career

- having a sense of daily accomplishment about your work

- having a sense of fulfilment from the career or job that you are in

- having the financial package you need to survive on and develop your preferred lifestyle from.

If you identify from the signs of occupational wellness that you may need to make some changes to improve yours, then here is a little introduction to some of the ways you can start to make those positive changes:

- Don't settle – use the other wellness dimensions to establish what you want and stay motivated in achieving it.

- Invest in your intellectual wellness and increase your knowledge and skills to accomplish your career goals through personal and professional development opportunities.

- Commit to some honest reflection on your role to identify the key benefits and positives in your current job.

- Create connections with your co-workers for a triple whammy because, alongside your occupational wellness, your social wellness and emotional wellness will improve too.

- Develop a career plan with clear goals and actions to meet and then actively work on them.

- Don't make the mistake of blaming employers, colleagues, family or friends. If you are unhappy, although others' actions may contribute to it, you are the only one who has the power to change it – you just have to make the decision and choice to do it.

What I hear too often from my clients is *'I am too old to try something new,' 'I am too institutionalised to go anywhere else,' 'Everyone wants a formal qualification,'* etc. etc., and my response is…*blah, blah, blah*. Don't misunderstand me: I don't mean to be rude or undermine their feelings, because I genuinely care, in fact, I care a lot about my clients, but I know that those reasons are falsehoods they tell themselves, just like I did, when they feel trapped and overwhelmed about having to make major life decisions that will lead to major life transitions.

Not one of the reasons I hear people use are 100% accurate or set in stone. In fact, they are inaccurate beliefs that create mental blockers, keeping people in their comfort zones because they are scared of trying something new.

Our self-esteem can lead us to believe that we are not worth the investment and that the hassles and challenges that may come with any changes would outweigh the positives. That belief is wrong; we are worth the investment and we can manage the challenges that come with transition, especially when they are positive for us.

Don't get me wrong, change is hard. It is difficult, it takes time, and it takes adjustment. But it is not impossible, and that uncomfortable transition period is for a limited time only. Once you are through that transition, you get the benefits, the happiness, he fulfilment and the self-esteem boost.

It may be helpful for me to share my experience. I always had a drive for success, but I never had the self-esteem or confidence levels needed to chase what I wanted. My own life experiences and self-belief prevented me from going to university at age eighteen along with my friends, and so I stayed back in the small country town I felt I was drowning in, in a job I detested, with a self-hatred that was growing daily.

How did I cope with that? I coped by throwing myself into what I call 'weekend binges'. In reality, those weekend binges were really Thursday to Monday most weeks.

What I did find when I stayed behind in that small town was a wonderful group of supportive people who eventually gave me the courage to take the plunge and move away before my increasingly poor decisions and behaviours led to something I would regret forever. *This is the power of social wellness, and why it is so important. A good social support system can change your life for better and I will go as far to say save your life too.*

I was twenty-two years old. I had no job, no money, no formal qualifications, no confidence, no self-esteem and, in my opinion, no prospects. What I did have was *Jagged Little Pill* by Alanis Morrisette on replay over and over in my head, filling me with angst, and a grandfather in Liverpool. And one day I finally made the call that changed my life. I asked my grandfather if I could come to Liverpool and stay for a while. Within one week I was there, changing my life. I was scared, I was lonely, I was out of my depth at first, but I soon got into the swing of things and with just my Liverpool A-Z, I started to create a new life for myself, which included a career too.

My grandfather often said to me in the years that followed that although I had said I was only staying for a short while, the second he saw me on his doorstep he knew I would never go back home, and he was right. I made Liverpool my home and that A-Z not only helped me navigate the big scary city but my life too. Those Liver Birds gave me some fire in my belly and enough confidence to put myself out there. This is the importance of environmental wellness – the right environment can ignite passion, can drive and motivate, whereas the wrong one can leave you fully deflated.

Here is my own personal timeline showing how my life changed:

- Within three days, I had an interview with a large Liverpool housing association as a financial administrator.

- Within two months, I had been accepted by the local college onto their counselling course.

- Within six months, that college offered me a student support role within their sparkly new arts college.

- Within three years, I was accepted into the University of Liverpool to study Criminology and Sociology.

- Within eight years, I was working for a large international corporate firm where I got the opportunity to become a senior manager, living in amazing cities such as London and Melbourne. I was even invited to speak at the House of Lords.

Within eight years, I went from zero to hero in my own life because I made one simple decision, no more blockers. The country girl was long gone, and although it took eight years to get there, each step along the journey had magical moments, new friends (who are still by my side to this day) and new experiences full of fun and frolics. Like everyone else, I experienced failures and successes that I learnt from, some I am still learning from to this day. The journey became more important than the destination – as cliché as that sounds, it is the truth. The journey brought me so many experiences, small wins, accomplishments and confidence, while the outcome brought me an overall sense of satisfaction and fulfilment. I was able to appreciate it all.

Now, I know what you might be thinking: *'Kim you did all this in your twenties, of course it was easier for you then – no kids, no mortgages etc.',* and you would be right. But things don't stay great forever unless you keep working at them, and life changed for me.

After an experience with workplace bullying, it wasn't too long before those old familiar thoughts came in. I hated my job, I hated the career I had developed, I was unfulfilled, my comfort zone was solid and guess what happened? Blockers! But along with the blockers were dysfunctional stress, anxiety and depression, plus a new range of life challenges and responsibilities too. My self-esteem was on the floor. I was unhappy in every sense of the word and in my opinion, firmly at rock bottom. The past fifteen years of my life had been built on my career and now that it wasn't working out. I felt like my world was crumbling around me and that I was crumbling on the inside too.

However, from my perspective, the best thing about being at rock bottom is there is only one place to go – up, and I am a firm believer that the harder the bottom, the bigger the bounce to the top. So, I made a decision, I chose me and my happiness, I started to stretch that comfort zone once again and I started to bounce.

In 2016, at the age of forty, I chose to take a career sabbatical for my mental health and here's what happened:

- Within six months, I was back in college studying to be a psychotherapist after making the decision to follow my passion of mental health and wellness that I had started nearly fifteen years previously when first moving to Liverpool.

- Within eighteen months, I started my own business using the skills and experience I had developed throughout my career and life itself to date and created 8Wise.

- Within two years, I quit my safe, senior management role within the corporate world to fully commit to my business, Dalton Wise.

- Within three years, I was fully qualified, with a thriving private practice.

- Within four years, I was being asked to be a guest speaker on podcasts, radio shows, at corporate events and as a guest blogger.

- Within five years, I wrote my first book ... this one.

I am living proof that you don't have to spend over 80,000 hours of your lifetime unhappy within your career or in a job that doesn't satisfy you. You can choose to make changes. You can choose to overcome challenges and you can choose to step outside your comfort zone – but only because you want to. Just because I did it doesn't mean you have to – you have your own path to take, but just be honest with yourself when you make those choices as to the real reason you are making them.

If you are unhappy in your career and your occupational wellness is suffering because of that, think about what small changes you can make that can improve your occupational wellness. Because the risk is if you don't, not only could you spend over 80,000 hours of your life unhappy, but your occupational wellness, or lack of it, could affect your other areas of wellness too. This in turn will have a huge impact on your mental and physical health – and is any job really worth damaging your health for?

A friend once said to me, 'You dedicate your life to a company, but if you died tomorrow, before you were buried in the ground, they would have job ads out to replace you; so, choose happiness over any company – they will never put you first, so you have to.'

So, get real with yourself, and use 8Wise to understand why you are choosing to stay unhappy, stuck and unfulfilled in your current job. Use it firstly to understand and acknowledge those blockers that are keeping you a prisoner in your own dysfunctional comfort zone, and then when ready, make the changes you need to improve your occupational wellness

Finally, for this segment, I want to make something perfectly clear to you, just in case you were doubting it or questioning it.

YOU ARE WORTH THE INVESTMENT!

Because otherwise, you will spend nearly 80,000 hours of your life unhappy, miserable, stressed, anxious, feeling unfulfilled, unappreciated, unmotivated, depressed and away from your loved ones. That's no way to spend a third of your life. That's not a life at all. Staying in an occupation that has such negative effects on your life may not feel like it, but it is a life choice. One that leads to poor mental and physical health, so if you can, make a better choice.

If you want to jump ahead to the action phase for Occupational Wellness go to the following pages:

Assessment page: 243
The Goal Setting Action Plan page: 207 & 285
Activities, tools and tips page: 251

When people say to me, 'I go to work to get paid,' I question it. I fully understand that the reason many people work is to have the financial reward that pays for the other things in life; it's part of our survival for most people. But we can't ignore that there are also people who choose to work even though they do not financially need to, and so is it possible that money and financial reward is not the only reason we go to work? I believe we get more out of work than just the financial reward and I believe the other reasons link to those outlined in 8Wise: purpose, interests and stimulation, social engagement, a different space. These also play their part in the reason for not only going to work every day but also where we choose to work every day.

I believe there is always more to the importance of something than just the most obvious reason. That is the same for money – there is more to it than the most obvious reason that we like to have it, which is because we need it to survive. Understanding these other reasons helps you to develop strong financial wellness, which brings us to the last element within 8Wise.

Financial Wellness

When I was at university, I had to work in order to survive and I worked as a debt recovery officer for a large financial firm. This role required me to help people manage their finances in order to repay any debts. I learnt a lot about money in the three years I worked there, and I even managed to get myself out of the financial mess I had gotten myself into (remember those bad choices I was making in life before leaving for Liverpool? Money mistakes were one of the big ones). The main thing that I learnt back then though was that there is one constant in life and that is that there is no escape from money. Or should I say it is highly unlikely you will be able to live a life where money is not a determining factor to the quality of your life, in one way or another. It is for this reason that 8Wise includes financial wellness in its approach.

For me, financial wellness refers to the relationship you have with money, both emotionally and practically. This includes how secure you are with money, currently and in the future, and what plans you have in the short, medium and long term to maintain that security. It also refers to the skills you have to manage your finances and what your overall attitude and beliefs are about money in general.

The four essential components for financial wellness within 8Wise are:

1. **Money**: Understanding what money means to you, as this is your motivator for financial wellness

2. **Financial literacy**: Having the skills and knowledge on different financial matters to be able to manage finances effectively

3. **Financial planning**: Understanding your current situation and having clear financial goals to be able to build a financial plan from

4. **Money management**: Having the tools, skills and systems to manage your finances effectively

So, let's start developing your financial wellness with the four essential components.

1. Money

What does money mean to you? That may seem like a simple question but take a minute to really think about it.

- Is it security for you or for your family?

- Is it a status symbol?

- Does it bring you freedom to live the lifestyle you want?

- Does it allow you to buy nice things to show to the world?

- Does it allow you to do charitable work to help and support others?

- Is it something completely different?

There is no right or wrong answer. The key is understanding what it means to you, so you can find satisfaction with your current or future financial situations. Which then means you can experience financial wellness. It also provides you with clarity as to what your financial driver is – we all have one, some people have more than one, and it can change over time. For example, in my youth my financial driver was status because I believed that if I had money, I would have status and affluent people would respect me which I believed would improve my self-esteem and confidence. This is, of course, not true and a tough lesson I learnt. This belief has since changed, and now for me personally, money means freedom – it allows me to have the freedom to live the life I want. Whatever that will be, and I accept the life I want is an everchanging variable as I adapt and grow as a person.

2. Financial literacy

You don't just need to understand what money means to you; you also need to understand the language of money. This means having the knowledge and skills to make effective decisions and develop money management tools. To do this you need to understand the following:

- the basics of creating and maintaining a budget, so you can have control over your finances

- understanding interest rates and the different aspects of them so you can make decisions about savings, loans, mortgages and investments. Some of this is complex maths and so if your maths is bad as my own is *(I retook my maths exam three times just to get a pass)* then I recommend you seek trusted advice

- the importance of savings for maintaining a healthy financial situation through to retirement

- credit and debit cycle traps including the difficulties and process for getting out of debt, as well as the difficulties associated with gaining, maintaining and re-gaining good credit

- having the ability to stay financially safe through preventative measures to protect against identify theft and fraud.

3. Financial Planning

We can't escape the planning required in life. 8Wise itself is built on the premise of developing a lifelong wellness plan for yourself, and planning financially is no different.

To make effective financial plans you need to take into consideration your current situation so that you can identify some clear goals and objectives for where you want your finances to be in the future and why. From this, you are then able to set a clear course of action to meet those goals with regular review and evaluation to ensure you remain on track, making amendments if and when required.

4. Money Management

I strongly encourage you to take control of your finances through good money management. This requires you to use all of the financial wellness components already stated to understand what your money priorities are to you. You then need to track your monthly income and expenditure through a budget that is in a format of your choice and is user-friendly for you. From your budget, you can then implement the financial plan previously covered and ensure you build in contingencies for emergencies. Don't forget to add savings on to that plan and tackle any debt, quickly. When you find an approach that works for your money management, stick with it and it will help with your financial wellness.

Now you might still be asking why financial wellness fits in with a mental wellness and wellbeing plan such as 8Wise, and the answer is simple…money and mental health are connected.

The stress of worrying about your money can lead to mental health issues, and mental health issues can lead to poor money management and reduce earning potential. It can become a vicious cycle – a cycle I want you to stay out of or get out of quickly with the help of the 8Wise approach.

Facing financial issues and sorting them out may feel daunting, overwhelming and scary, but if you follow the steps at a pace that is right for you, you can gain control of your finances and develop financial wellness too.

Financial wellness also involves the process of learning how to successfully manage financial expenses, emotionally and rationally. This is important for your overall wellness and wellbeing because money plays a critical role in our lives, and not having enough of it or control over it impacts your health as well as your desired lifestyle.

Through my work as both a debt collector and psychotherapist, and also through my own personal experience with money difficulties, I understand that finances are a common point of stress for many of us. So, with 8Wise the aim is to minimise the worries about this aspect of your life and support you to implement the management tools and techniques that help limit the negative impact that any unsatisfactory finances may have on the other wellness dimensions. By taking control of this you can have positive balance across all eight elements.

We can't escape money, but we can escape the stress and anxiety that it brings through an effective financial wellness plan that supports with your overall health and wellbeing – which is the 8Wise way.

> *If you want to jump ahead to the action phase for Financial Wellness go to the following pages:*
>
> Assessment page: 246
> The Goal Setting Action Plan page: 207 & 285
> Activities, tools and tips page: 251

How to Use 8Wise

So, you have been introduced and provided with a good base knowledge of the four dimensions of the 8Wise approach and the eight elements that make up what I call your wellness spectrum – what's next?

Now, from my experience you are one of three types of person:

Person one – You have read through everything in this book in order and are now ready and motivated to take the next step and start developing your 8Wise plan using some effective tools and techniques from the final section of the book.

Person two – You have read through each dimension one at a time, jumping directly to the 8Wise practical activities in the final section for each dimension and so are close to completing your final 8Wise action plan.

Person three – You have read the book, and for whatever reasons have no intentions of doing the practical elements at this stage.

No matter what person you are I have a message for you:

Person one, well done, you now have the knowledge, so let's put it into action.

Person two, how is it going so far? Are you noticing any differences yet? Don't forget, you can always go back and re-read chapters if you need to.

Person three, maybe the time is not right for you at the moment, but 8Wise will be here when you are ready, no matter when that is.

No matter which person you are I hope you have learnt something beneficial for your life from the 8Wise approach. I hope it has led you to do some self-reflection and triggered some positive thinking processes for you.

8Wise was born out of my own experiences of depression and poor mental health. For me it has been the positive outcome from what I perceived to be one of the worst times in my life. But alongside my own experience I also developed it using my professional knowledge and experience, additional research and input from psychology specialists.

I wanted to develop the ultimate guide for a happy and healthy life. I wanted it to be simple, straight to the point with a step-by-step process that didn't dictate your journey but rather provided you with the framework to create your own journey, so that you can fulfil your real potential.

You may often hear, *'Strive to be the best version of yourself.'* I don't align to this way of thinking. I believe you should accept that you are always evolving – that's the meaning of life, after all – and so if you learn to know yourself and can learn to confidently live an authentic life because you know, understand and accept yourself, then you simply need to manage the version of yourself you are today with compassion, understanding, wisdom and balance.

Whether you are one of the 'one in four' experiencing mental health issues, or one of 'the other three', I hope 8Wise can support you to improve your wellness and wellbeing for a happier, healthier and more fulfilling life.

If you would like to continue your journey past this book, then come and join the 8Wise community, a safe space for people who are getting wise about their wellness and wellbeing the 8Wise way.

The 8Wise community can be found on:

Facebook: @8Wise

Instagram: @8wisekim

Website: www.daltonwise.co.uk

PART THREE

Your 8Wise Journey

Chapter 10:

Creating Your 8Wise Transition Plan

This is where the fun really starts. I hope you have enjoyed learning about the 8Wise approach for managing wellness and wellbeing. I hope it has triggered thoughts, feelings and some basic understanding of past and present experiences, as well as highlighting any issues you may have had or may be having currently regarding any of those eight core elements.

What I really hope is that you are motivated to take action and to make positive change. In order to use 8Wise as either a prevention method or recovery method for your mental health and wellbeing, it will take more than just having a better understanding of the four dimensions of the model and the core eight elements. Like everything else in life, thinking and researching only gets you so far – it's the land of good intentions, but it's actually the 'doing' that makes the difference – the practical process of implementing those teachings, learnings and knowledge into your life and your daily routine is what 8Wise is really all about. It is designed to help you to develop the tools that support you in gaining balance across your wellness spectrum for better mental health and wellbeing.

So far, I have shared with you the underpinning knowledge of wellness and wellbeing and the 8Wise approach, but now we move to the final part of this book: the action plan, personal coaching, self-development, personalisation, 'stop making excuses' and the 'let's get shit done' stages!

Welcome to your 8Wise Journey.

Your 8Wise Journey

Life does not stay still; sometimes that alone is the issue we may have, as life and the challenges it throws at us can move at a pace we are not quite ready for, hence the increased levels of stress and burnout we may experience at times. Instead, life is constantly moving and so to truly survive and grow we have to move with it. That is what 8Wise does – it gives you the tools to steer your ship (your life) towards optimal health and wellbeing, because life is not plain sailing and the events in life will challenge your mental health from time to time. No one survives unscathed – we all experience difficulties, high emotions, low moods and traumas – and with this in mind, I needed to create a methodology, model, and process that moved with you, especially when you find life experiences moving you towards mental health issues.

This is why I created 8Wise, and why I call it the 8Wise Journey: to support with both prevention and recovery, because it is likely you will need a support system for both within your lifetime.

Before you move on to the exciting part, where the magic happens, I first want to introduce you to some of the core tools you will use throughout your 8Wise Journey.

1. 8Wise Evaluation: This is where you establish your starting point. After all, if you want to move from 'A' to 'B', you need to identify 'A', your starting point. The 8Wise Evaluation process examines your current wellness and wellbeing levels to provide you with the information you need to make effective decisions for implementing positive change for your wellness and wellbeing.

2. 8Wise Map: This is the complete picture of where you are starting from and is used as the navigation tool for your 8Wise Journey, the compass that guides you towards those milestones.

3. 8Wise Milestone 1: A specific and achievable point you want to achieve within twelve weeks of your 8Wise Journey that measures the short-term progress you have made.

4. 8Wise Milestone 2: A specific and achievable point you want to achieve within six months of your 8Wise Journey that measures the mid-term progress you have made.

5. 8Wise Milestone 3: A specific and achievable point you want to achieve within twelve months of your 8Wise Journey that measures the long-term progress you have made.

6. 8Wise Steps: The detailed elements for the course of action you will take to meet each of the milestones you set for yourself on your 8Wise Journey.

7. 8Wise Transition Plan: The working document where you record each element of you 8Wise Journey (evaluation scores, milestones and steps).

8. 8Wise Review: The purpose of the review is to evaluate whether your 8Wise Journey and the objectives on your 8Wise Transition plan are met, determine how effective the process has been so far, identify lifelong lessons for the future 8Wise Transition plan, take accountability where needed, and to set future milestones for the benefit of your long-term mental and physical health.

Developing your 8Wise Transition Plan

Although from the list above the 8Wise transition plan is only listed as point seven, because the process is leading to this point I wanted to start by explaining it in a little more detail.

By now you will have realised I like to make sure there is clarity in the subjects and topics I cover, and it is no different in this part of the book. Let's start with what a transition plan is, because from my experience with my own clients, it gets confused between 'check list' and 'goals'. The truth is that a transition plan is both of these plus a little bit more too. It is a checklist for the steps you need to complete in order to achieve the milestones you set for yourself in your life. Note I say milestones and not goals, and that's because from my perspective the goal is already set – 'Improve your wellness and wellbeing to protect your mental and physical health for a happier, healthier and more fulfilling life'. 8Wise has been developed to move you towards that goal and I recommend you set milestones that keep you focused throughout the journey towards that goal.

Example: For me personally to be healthy and happy I would like to learn to run 5k and 10k races *(this is actually a personal truth of mine – I am not a long-distance runner and I get really jealous in the spring and summer watching people running freely around my local park – not so much in the winter though)*. On my 8Wise Transition plan I record this as a timebound milestone, with the steps I need to complete to get there. On the plan it would look a little like this:

Milestone 1: To be able to run 5k within three months

- Step 1: Download the 'Couch to 5k' App

- Step 2: Buy some suitable running shoes and clothing

- Step 3: Schedule diary for running time

- Step 4: Complete the Couch to 5K plan

Now this is just a taster of the content of your 8Wise Transition Plan, because when it comes to building an effective plan, it really needs to include the following components:

1. Milestones that are clear and concise

2. Steps to ensure you meet your milestones

3. Prioritising your milestones and steps to create time-lines for completion

4. Resource and support required to complete each of the steps

5. Tangible measures to evaluate your progress

6. Processes to review and evaluate the plan.

What's great about having an 8Wise Transition Plan is that everything is listed down in one place which makes it easier to track your progress and adapt it where necessary. An 8Wise Transition Plan is not something set in stone because as you move through it, and as your wellness and wellbeing improves, you may find that your priorities change. Your milestones may change too, and so your 8Wise Transition Plan will change along with it. Therefore, the 8Wise Transition Plan is a document and process that needs to be revisited and evaluated regularly to keep it up to date with your changing life, your needs, and your milestones.

But other than tracking progress, what else is 8Wise Transition Plan good for? The answer is planning. Because life is not linear, and as we have identified, many stress triggers come from external factors and life events that are outside of your control. So, you will have to be in a mindset to 'respond' effectively and you need to be your own response unit. Planning helps you prepare for those challenges and obstacles; it creates a framework for you to respond with that keeps things manageable and on track. With an effective 8Wise Transition Plan, you can boost your productivity, keep yourself focused, and improve your wellness and wellbeing.

Here are some benefits of an 8Wise Transition Plan.

- It gives you a clear direction as it highlights exactly what steps are to be taken and when they should be completed, helping you to know exactly what you need to do.

- Having your milestones written down and planned out in steps will give you a reason to stay motivated and committed throughout the process.

- You can track your progress toward your milestones.

- Listing down all the steps you need to complete will help you prioritise your steps based on effort and impact.

Creating your 8Wise Transition Plan is an essential part of your 8Wise Journey, and through the rest of the book I will help you do exactly that – create your own 8Wise Transition Plan for you to manage your own wellness and wellbeing.

8Wise Evaluation and Map

I have said many times to my clients, and now I want to say it to you, that I see 8Wise as putting you firmly in the driving seat of your personal journey towards optimal mental and physical health, by improving wellness and wellbeing. Just like any successful journey, 8Wise guides you to plan your wellness and wellbeing journey in stages. Stage one starts with establishing exactly where you are starting from, because on any journey there is no getting from 'A' to 'B', if there is no 'A' to begin with.

To establish your 'A' you need to complete the 8Wise Evaluation.

In the following chapter you will find an 8Wise Evaluation for all eight elements of the 8Wise model, plus useful tips to get your mind twitching with ideas with regards to what your milestones or steps might be. By completing each evaluation, you will be able to score yourself out of eight, and you then plot each score on to the 8Wise map. The scoring is between 1 and 8, with 1 being a low score and 8 being a high score. When it is completed, it should look a little like the diagram.

The key to any self-reflection and self-evaluation is be honest with your answers. Answer them based on who or where you are right now in your life – *now*, not who or where you *want* to be. If you establish an accurate starting place, a point 'A', then it is more likely the steps that follow will help you be more successful in completing your milestones.

Diagram 1: Example of a completed 8Wise Map shows that this person has scored highly on intellectual wellness with a score of 8, but low on spiritual wellness and emotional wellness with only a score of 2.

When your 8Wise Map is completed, you will be able to identify the elements which you scored lowest and those you scored highest. This helps you to identify which areas you should prioritise over others to start with.

Based on the 8Wise Map above, this person would start by focussing on the lower results: Emotional, Spiritual, Physical and Financial, as these results are 50% or less of the maximum score available. I always recommend starting with one or two elements at a time as not to overwhelm yourself with too much change.

With your completed 8Wise Map, you can then move on and start creating your 8Wise Transition plan following the process covered in this chapter and the tasks I have provided to help you meet your goals in the chapters to come … this is the start of your 8Wise journey and, more importantly, your healthier and happier life.

Your 8Wise Map template

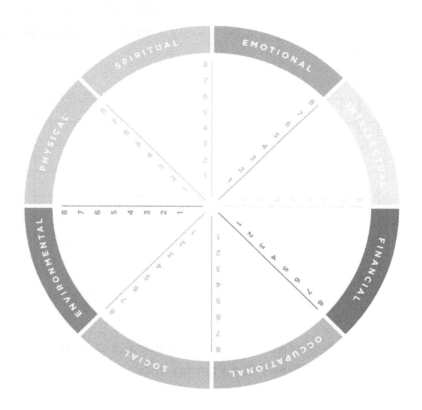

When you have completed all eight evaluations, you will have a score for each of the elements. You will then plot each score on your 8Wise Map, as the example showed you previously. When you are able to see all eight scored together on your 8Wise Map, you then need to identify which ones to start improving first. In the table below, prioritise the elements; your lowest score should be priority 1 and your highest score priority 8.

1	
2	
3	
4	
5	
6	
7	
8	

So, get comfy, get hydrated, get reflective and start developing your own 8Wise Transition Plan for improving your wellness and wellbeing.

8Wise Milestones and Steps

For these pages, I want to break it down into three stages, and use the 8Wise Transition Plan template on page …

Stage One: Milestones

For your 8Wise Transition Plan you will need to set three milestones that you want to achieve, and these must be timebound:

- **Milestone one:** a short-term goal that you can achieve within three months

- **Milestone two:** a mid-term goal that you can achieve within six months

- **Milestone three:** a long-term goal that you can achieve within twelve months

8W Insight: Did you know it takes 21 days to create a new habit and 90 days to create a new lifestyle? With 8Wise, your aim is to create a new lifestyle, which is why milestone one, your short-term milestone, is a three-month focus, because three months is also approximately 90 days.

As I have already explained, we know that life will throw you obstacles and curve balls, and so with 8Wise we focus on one year at a time, reviewing your transition plan every three months to see if you need to make changes and adapt it to keep you on track for achieving those goals you set.

Now, before you jump in with listing three milestones, there is a final expectation of the milestones you set – they must pass quality control.

Quality control, when it comes to goal setting, usually means being S.M.A.R.T. – an acronym with each letter representing a specific requirement for the goal to meet: *Specific, Measurable, Attainable, Relevant, Timebound.* For the majority of my career, it has been a standard process to follow within personal and professional development. But this is the 8Wise Wellness Journey, and a more efficient way to quality-check the milestones you put in place for yourself is to move F.A.S.T. – an acronym, like S.M.A.R.T, but with the letters representing *Focus, Ambitious, Specific and Truthful* instead. The original word for 'F' was Frequent, and 'T' was Transparent, which are both still important, but more relevant when setting goals for others to follow. I have adapted them to Focus and Truthful because they are more relevant to the type of personal milestones and steps you will be setting for yourself.

First, you need to assess where you are now. You will get an opportunity to do that in the next few chapters through the 8Wise evaluation, where you will be able to assess yourself against the eight elements of the 8Wise model.

From there, you will be able to start identifying where you want to be in comparison to where you are now.

The next step then is to identify the core problem, or problems, causing your current state and start mapping out what you think the solutions might be. For example, if your physical wellness is low then maybe you want to start implementing a more active lifestyle or focus on your sleep. But remember, fully analyse the situation before jumping in on what you think is the obvious solution, or you might prioritise your milestones ineffectively.

When you have decided on your milestone, you then need to run it through quality control, which in this case is F.A.S.T. This means checking that the milestones you set for yourself tick each of the F.A.S.T. quality check points – think of it as the checks that happen on a Formula1 car before it heads out to race.

The diagram below explains the F.A.S.T. model for you.

F	Focus	It should have a clear focus that ensures your commitment and motivation. Questions to ask yourself: • What do I want? • Why do I want it? • How motivated am I on a scale of 1 to 10 to achieve it?
A	Ambitious	It should be realistic but should take you out of your comfort zone for growth. Questions to ask yourself: • Does this challenge me? • Do I have to learn new things? • Is it realistic to achieve?
S	Specific	There should be clarity on what you are trying to achieve and measures that confirm it. Questions to ask yourself: • Do you have clear actions? • Do you have clear timelines? • Do you have clear progress and achievement measures?
T	Truthful	It should be authentic to you and what you want to achieve and not set by someone else. Questions to ask yourself: • Is it clear about what I have to do? • Is it clear within what timeframe I should achieve it? • Does it have a clear measure in place that confirms my progress and success in achieving it?

When your milestones have passed through the F.A.S.T. quality control check, you can then move onto the next stage – 8Wise Steps.

Stage Two: Steps

I was once asked by the CEO of the international corporate company I worked for if I could turn their number one best-selling book into a training course to deliver to a group of VIP guests we had visiting one of our offices in London. The ambitious and driven woman in me said 'yes' without getting any important details such as, what timeframe did I have, when would I get access to the book and who were the VIPs? That information came to me later in the day, which was a Friday at 5pm and we finished work at 5:30pm – I nearly had a mini meltdown. I was told I had eight days to read the book, understand the core concepts then turn them into a fully branded three-day training product that included all interactive learner materials and workbooks, trainers' guides, slides and video recordings, which would be delivered to a team of Westminster MPs.

At that stage, I had never seen the book, and I was due to be at Twickenham all weekend watching the rugby with my family (a huge annual family event that I could not get out of) and so would not have the weekend to prepare either. So, as I could feel the pressure building up in my chest, my breathing started to change, and the nausea kicked in, I suddenly remembered what my manager once said to me when we had been tasked before with a gargantuan project with intense deadlines.

She had said to me on a very rainy day in Tottenham, North London, 'Kim, how do you eat an elephant?' I must have looked at her as if she had lost the plot because she smiled a cheeky smile and whispered, 'In bite size chunks, and that's how you tackle this'. So, with this new project I did exactly that. I broke it down into bite size chunks, or what I like to call steps, because steps move you forward, or upwards, and that's what any good plan should support you to do.

I first identified the process that I needed to follow to complete this project end to end. I then identified each problem that linked to each stage of the process and then developed a solution. Was it a tough project to complete? Yes. Did I complete it? Yes. Did I do it alone? No, because it is unlikely when we have any big project to complete that we can do it alone, and I wasn't naïve enough to even try. We met our deadline, we delivered that training, the MPs gave great feedback, and that training course remained in the business for a few more years – I even got the chance to deliver it to inmates in Wandsworth Prison.

So, what is the point of this little trip down my memory lane? Well, it isn't to show off about my accomplishments, although I was very proud of what we had achieved. It was to make the point that your wellness and wellbeing is a gigantic project, and if you were to try and tackle it in one big lump, it is likely to overwhelm you. You could risk potential burnout which could lead to demotivation and then, if you are anything like I used to be, you might give up, and then deem this as another failure about which you beat yourself up over for weeks, months, and years to come. Of course, you might simply accept that it was just a poorly executed plan, dust yourself off and create a more effective action plan next time, which is a better response. Or you could go with the third option, or what should really be the first option, which is create a transition plan that is built on smaller steps that will move you towards those milestones and towards that ultimate goal, to *'Improve your wellness and wellbeing to protect your mental and physical health for a happier, healthier and more fulfilling life'* – that's the 8Wise way to eat your elephant.

Just like with your milestones, make sure that each step is F.A.S.T. through the same quality control process as before, and if obstacles and challenges show up that make the steps more complex, simply treat them like an elephant in their own right and break them down to smaller steps that are easier to execute and manage.

Stage Three: Prioritising

Not all steps and milestones are equal. Not all need to be completed at the same time and some need to be completed before others can even start. So prioritising your steps and milestones effectively is a crucial component for an effective 8Wise Transition Plan.

- Start by writing all of your steps down – using sticky notes is a good way to do this activity.

- Write one step per sticky note and then line all the sticky notes up in order of when they need to be completed to meet the goal. Remember to pay attention to steps that must be completed in a specific order. For example, you can't have a shower if you haven't undressed yet! Well, you can but it is likely to just add more work and inconvenience to your life!

- When this is done, working backwards from the deadlines you have set for your overall goals, add a realistic timeline and deadline for each step listed and then add everything onto your transition plan.

Now you have milestones set, steps set, and deadlines too. You almost have a perfect 8Wise transition plan.

Stage Four: Resources and support

No person is an island, my friend, and although sometimes it may seem easier to do everything alone, it rarely is. When you look at each of the elements within 8Wise, you can see that additional resources at each stage may be beneficial and required. I have laid some potential options out in the table on the following page.

Resources and support

Element	Example
Emotional Wellness	friends, colleagues, employer, family, counsellor, coach, partner
Physical Wellness	friends, colleagues, employer, family, personal trainer, weight loss group, doctor, dentist, partner
Spiritual Wellness	friends, colleagues, family, counsellor, coach, religious leader, partner
Intellectual Wellness	friends, colleagues, family, counsellor, coach, educational practitioner, interest group, partner
Environmental Wellness	friends, colleagues, family, employer, estate agents, tradesmen, partner
Social Wellness	friends, colleagues, employer, family, community leaders, partner
Occupational Wellness	friends, colleagues, employer, family, community leaders, career coach, recruitment agents, partner
Financial Wellness	friends, employer, family, bank, financial advisor, educational practitioner, partner

These examples are a quick way to demonstrate that you will no doubt need additional resources throughout your 8Wise journey. It may come in the guise of practical support or simply emotional support, but either way, when making life changes you need to include others, and so you need to identify who, when and how you might need them so you can account for it within your 8Wise transition plan.

Don't forget to include your budget too – as we know, very little comes for free in this world, and some of the resources you will want or need to help you reach your milestones will have a cost attached to them. Go in with open eyes regarding your finances and make sure they play a part in whether your plans are F.A.S.T.

Stage Five: Tangible Measures

How will you know if you have succeeded with each step, as a deadline is not enough? The answer is tangible measures, the facts and specific outcomes that confirm you have successfully completed that step.

For example, if it is weight loss it may be the pounds or kilograms on the scale. If it's learning, it may be a qualification and certificate, and if it's financial it may be a debt paid off or a specific amount saved in the bank account. Whatever it is, you need to include these tangible measures, because measurables equate to motivation. Not having measurables will lead to demotivation, and you know where demotivation can lead to *(a little clue: it's the opposite of success)*, and no one wants that when it comes to your wellness and wellbeing.

Step Six: Process to Review and Evaluate

The world is ever changing. Your life is ever changing, your circumstances could be ever changing, and as a person you are ever changing, because you are evolving. Therefore an effective transition plan must be flexible to those changes. But if you don't review it regularly and ensure it is up-to-date with you and your life then it will not align with you, and your milestones will be unachievable because they are no longer realistic or relevant.

I recommend reviewing your whole 8Wise Transition Plan a minimum of every three months, or more regularly if possible. Allocate some time to evaluate the progress you've made and adapt the 8Wise Transition Plan if needed.

The 8Wise Transition Plan is designed to guide your way to accomplishing your wellness and wellbeing goals. It turns your health and happiness vision into clear actions that lead to clear and tangible goals and will help keep you motivated, focussed and on track.

The following pages provide you with all the tools needed to create your first 8Wise Transition Plan plus some exercises that can help you with each of the elements within the 8Wise core dimensions. You can start improving your wellness and wellbeing immediately and start protecting your mental and physical health for the long-term.

As I said earlier, I created 8Wise as a model that puts you firmly back in the driving seat for your own wellness and wellbeing. Therefore the process outlined in this book is just a guide; you don't have to follow it. You can use the 8Wise dimensions in any way you feel would benefit your mental health and wellbeing – after all, this is your life and so this has to be your 8Wise Journey.

I regularly create new tools and exercises that you can access through my social media accounts and website so you can keep building your own 8Wise tool kit.

www.daltonwise.co.uk

www.instagram.com/8wisekim

www.facebook.com/8wise

Chapter 11:

Creating Your 8Wise Map

So, let us begin … as explained, we start the 8Wise journey by establishing the position we are currently starting from – not where we were, not where we wish we were, but where we actually are. It's time to face the fear and really reflect and evaluate where your wellness is against all eight elements.

Below are evaluations for each of the eight elements with a short recap to help you focus on the questions. Answer each question honestly, you are only cheating yourself if you don't. You want to start from a position of authenticity to achieve milestones that are realistic and relevant to your life, your wellness, your wellbeing and your mental health.

There are ten questions in each evaluation, each rated 1 to 4 as described below:

- Never   1
- Rarely   2
- Sometimes   3
- Usually   4

Simply:

- Circle the number in the column that most represents you

- Tally up each column

- Calculate your overall total.

The overall total corresponds with an 8Wise plot number. Write this on your 8Wise Map and watch it come to life with an overall evaluation of your wellness and wellbeing from which to navigate your 8Wise Journey.

FOUNDATION DIMENSION: Emotional Wellness

Recap: Emotional wellness involves your ability to cope with stress, express emotions, and feel positive about your life. People with healthy emotional wellness feel confident, in control of their feelings and behaviours, build satisfying relationships with others, can handle life challenges, and can love themselves and others.

Complete the following assessment to identify your current level of emotional wellness and start to fill in your 8Wise Map.

Emotional Wellness Evaluation

	Question	Rate yourself			
		Never	Rarely	Sometimes	Usually
1	I find it easy to express a wide range of emotions constructively	1	2	3	4
2	I am can bounce back after a disappointment or problem	1	2	3	4
3	I feel I have tools to manage stress	1	2	3	4
4	I am able to set priorities and make decisions with minimal stress or negative thoughts and feelings	1	2	3	4
5	I feel good about myself and who I am as a person	1	2	3	4
6	I am able to adapt to life challenges and transitions positively	1	2	3	4
7	I am able to maintain a positive balance between work, family, friends and other obligations	1	2	3	4
8	I think before I act	1	2	3	4
9	I accept responsibility for my own thoughts, beliefs and behaviours	1	2	3	4
10	I am happy to ask for help when I need it	1	2	3	4
Totals					
Total Score					/40

8Wise Map Score board

Using the total score for the assessment, find your score in row A of the table below, then identify your corresponding 8Wise plot number in row B.

Plot this number on your 8Wise Map to represent your score for this section

A	10	11 - 15	16 - 20	21 - 25	25 - 30	31 - 35	36 - 39	40
B	1	2	3	4	5	6	7	8

My Top 5 Emotional Wellness tips to consider when identifying your 8Wise Steps for your 8Wise Transition plan.

1 Awareness of Thoughts and Feelings: Take time to become aware of certain thoughts or triggers that cause negative emotions.

2 Staying Positive: Noticing how often you think or say negative things is the first step towards having a positive attitude – then work on limiting them.

3 Ask for Help: Seeking support doesn't mean you are weak; it means you are strong enough to take care of your mental health.

4 Keep Boundaries: Establishing boundaries with people in your life will keep you from feeling overwhelmed by other people's expectations and behaviours.

5 Self-Acceptance: Becoming aware and then learning how to manage negative thoughts and self-talk is key to learning how to accept yourself.

Summary: Your emotional wellness is the key to your mental wellness, so put time and effort into improving it and maintaining it for optimum health and wellbeing. Don't fall victim to the most common reason for not implementing an effective self-care practice, which is 'no time'. Be honest with yourself – what is more important than your mental and physical health, your survival, your life? The answer should be nothing, and if it isn't then you are more at risk of damaging your longer-term mental and physical health than you realise.

FOUNDATION DIMENSION: Physical Wellness

Recap: Physical Wellness is about healthy habits regarding physical activity, a nutritious diet, adequate sleep, appropriate health care, practicing safe behaviours, and overall physical health.

Complete the assessment below to identify your current level of physical wellness and fill in your 8Wise Map.

Physical Wellness Evaluation

	Question	Never	Rarely	Sometimes	Usually
				Rate yourself	
1	I protect myself from getting ill	1	2	3	4
2	I eat a nutritionally balanced diet	1	2	3	4
3	I engage in regular exercise	1	2	3	4
4	I get enough hours of sleep each night	1	2	3	4
5	I seek professional help when I feel something is wrong physically	1	2	3	4
6	I use alcohol responsibly (including avoiding binge drinking, drink driving)	1	2	3	4
7	I avoid using tobacco and other drugs (including both over the counter and illicit)	1	2	3	4
8	I maintain a desirable healthy weight	1	2	3	4
9	I practice safe sex practices	1	2	3	4
10	I stay hydrated	1	2	3	4
	Totals				
	Total Score				/40

8Wise Map Score board

Using the total score for the assessment, find your score in row A of the table below, then identify your corresponding 8Wise plot number in row B.

Plot this number on your 8Wise Map to represent your score for this section

A	10	11 - 15	16 - 20	21 - 25	25 - 30	31 - 35	36 - 39	40
B	1	2	3	4	5	6	7	8

My Top 5 Physical Wellness tips to consider when identifying your 8Wise Steps for your 8Wise Transition plan.

1 Sleep: Your body craves a regular routine especially when it comes to sleep. Create a routine that works for you with the aim of 7-9 hours sleep.

2 Eating Well: A routine of eating vegetables, fruits, lean meats and whole grains gives your body the nutrients for better function, and for balancing your mental well-being as well.

3 Physical Exercise: A routine of daily exercise has both short-term and long-term benefits to your wellness and well-being; aim for 30 minutes a day of an activity you enjoy.

4 Hygiene: Hygiene includes both personal care and preventative medical care, so stay clean and fresh daily, and don't put off those health checks.

5 Relaxation: Whether it is getting a massage, staying home with a good book or playing your favourite sport, some 'me time' does everyone good.

Summary: Your physical wellness links with your emotional wellness and has an effect on your mental health, so it is important to give it the adequate focus it needs. Don't make the mistake of thinking aches and pains don't mean anything. You need to learn to know your body and how it functions, what it reacts well to and what it doesn't. Your body is a vessel, and it needs optimum physical wellness to keep it functioning properly and moving your forward in your life, so do all you can to maintain and protect it.

INTERNAL DIMENSIONS: Spiritual Wellness

Recap: Spiritual wellness is related to your values and beliefs that help you find meaning and purpose in your life. Strong signs of spiritual health include having clear values, a sense of compassion, and a feeling of inner peace.

Complete the assessment below to identify your current level of spiritual wellness and fill in your 8Wise Map.

Spiritual Wellness Evaluation

	Question	Rate yourself			
		Never	Rarely	Sometimes	Usually
1	I take time to think about what is important in my life	1	2	3	4
2	I make time for relaxation every day	1	2	3	4
3	I feel like my life has purpose and meaning	1	2	3	4
4	I show my life values through my actions	1	2	3	4
5	I feel connected to something larger than myself (nature, humanity, community, supreme being)	1	2	3	4
6	I have found a balance between meeting my needs and meeting the needs of others	1	2	3	4
7	I appreciate the deeper meanings to life	1	2	3	4
8	I accept the views, values and beliefs of others	1	2	3	4
9	I am able to show empathy and sympathy towards others	1	2	3	4
10	I understand who I am and accept who I am (including values, beliefs and purpose)	1	2	3	4
Totals					
Total Score					/40

8Wise Map Score board

Using the total score for the assessment, find your score in row A of the table below, then identify your corresponding 8Wise plot number in row B.

Plot this number on your 8Wise Map to represent your score for this section

A	10	11 - 15	16 - 20	21 - 25	25 - 30	31 - 35	36 - 39	40
B	1	2	3	4	5	6	7	8

My Top 5 Spiritual Wellness tips to consider when identifying your 8Wise Steps for your 8Wise Transition plan.

1 Values and Beliefs: Understand yourself; what are the values and core beliefs that drive you. How do they reflect on you behaviours?

2 Purpose: Reflect on your purpose - how does it align with your values, beliefs and behaviours? Reflect on your identify and feel confident in your choices.

3 Self-Acceptance: Learn to accept yourself for who you are not who you wish you were. You are unique, so be confident in who you are and the choices you make in life.

4 Gratitude: Being grateful for what you have in life that brings you joy and peace will help bring calm, clarity and inner strength.

5 Be Mindful: Living in the moment teaches you to appreciate life and all its everyday pleasures and curiosities.

Summary: If you don't know who you are, how will anyone else? If you don't know who you are, how will you ever know what you want in life, what you believe in, what you stand for, who your 'pack' of people are and what your purpose is? That is the power of spiritual wellness – it embeds the core elements of your identity into all of your interactions in your life, through your values and beliefs, which then manifests into your behaviours, drivers and purpose.

Your spiritual wellness is what calms your inner world so that you can engage with the external world on your terms with confidence, healthy self-esteem and true authenticity. Your spiritual wellness is the foundation for you to develop an effective response system that manages the chaos in life in and protects your mental health.

INTERNAL DIMENSION: Intellectual Wellness

Recap: Intellectual wellness is when you recognise and accept your own talents and seek out new knowledge and skills in creative ways for mental growth and personal development. Intellectual wellness can improve concentration, attention and critical thinking skills.

Complete the assessment below to identify your current level of intellectual wellness and fill in your 8Wise Map.

Intellectual Wellness Evaluation

	Question	Never	Rarely	Sometimes	Usually
1	I seek personal growth by learning new skills and gaining new knowledge	1	2	3	4
2	Before making decisions, I gather facts	1	2	3	4
3	I seek ways to use my critical thinking skills	1	2	3	4
4	I look for ways to use my creative skills	1	2	3	4
5	I make an effort to keep up-to-date with current affairs	1	2	3	4
6	I enjoy sharing knowledge with others	1	2	3	4
7	I manage my time well, rather than it managing me	1	2	3	4
8	I seek out weekly mental stimulation via magazines, books or other media	1	2	3	4
9	I am open to new ideas and the ideas of others	1	2	3	4
10	I value a life-long learning approach	1	2	3	4
	Totals				
	Total Score				/40

8Wise Map Score board

Using the total score for the assessment, find your score in row A of the table below, then identify your corresponding 8Wise plot number in row B.

Plot this number on your 8Wise Map to represent your score for this section

A	10	11 - 15	16 - 20	21 - 25	25 - 30	31 - 35	36 - 39	40
B	1	2	3	4	5	6	7	8

My Top 5 Intellectual Wellness tips to consider when identifying your 8Wise Steps for your 8Wise Transition plan.

1 Read for Fun: Reading, especially something you enjoy, can improve your intellect by stretching your mind to think about things you normally don't think about!

2 Podcasts: Podcasts are also excellent ways to learn about new topics you may be interested in.

3 Learn a New Skill: Whether it's cooking, gardening, crafting or building, learning a new skill is a fun and interactive way to improve your intellectual intelligence.

4 Time Management: Poor time management can lead to increased stress, which affects all wellness areas. Being organised allows your mind to work more efficiently and effectively.

5 Create: Similar to the positive effects of reading, being creative is known to improve memory retention as well as emotional stability.

Summary: As I have said from the beginning, we have an inbuilt system to retain information and an ability to learn from it. Thanks to our subconscious, we are able to store information for longer periods, until a time when we might need to recall it. These brain functions are what lead to our intellectual development.

How we choose to develop can vary from person to person based on our own intellectual abilities, so it's important that you not only understand what interests you but also how you learn in order to get the best experience from expanding your knowledge and skills.

Boredom can be a trigger for mental health issues, as can a sense of 'being stuck', not developing and not evolving. It is important to identify the things that mentally stimulate you and engage with them as often as possible, hence the need for hobbies, but it is equally important to push yourself out of your comfort zone and learn new things in creative ways.

EXTERNAL DIMENSION: Environmental Wellness

Recap: Environmental wellness relates to your external surroundings; your social environment and your natural environment play a part as both are entwined with each other. Our environments can impact how we feel, think and behave.

Complete the assessment below to identify your current level of environmental wellness and fill in your 8Wise Map.

Environmental Wellness Evaluation

	Question	Never	Rarely	Sometimes	Usually
			Rate yourself		
1	I recognise the impact of my actions on my environment	1	2	3	4
2	I recognise the impact specific environments have on my mood and health	1	2	3	4
3	I spend time regularly in spaces that I love	1	2	3	4
4	I spend time outdoors enjoying nature	1	2	3	4
5	I surround myself with a social environment that has a positive impact on my health	1	2	3	4
6	I make efforts to reduce my carbon footprint	1	2	3	4
7	I have created a safe space for rest, relaxation and self-reflection	1	2	3	4
8	I keep spaces clean and clutter-free	1	2	3	4
9	I have an element of nature inside my living and working environments	1	2	3	4
10	I get to choose how the spaces I live and work in are laid out and/or decorated.	1	2	3	4
	Totals				
	Total Score				/40

8Wise Map Score board

Using the total score for the assessment, find your score in row A of the table below, then identify your corresponding 8Wise plot number in row B.

Plot this number on your 8Wise Map to represent your score for this section

A	10	11 - 15	16 - 20	21 - 25	25 - 30	31 - 35	36 - 39	40
B	1	2	3	4	5	6	7	8

My Top 5 Environmental Wellness tips to consider when identifying your 8Wise Steps for your 8Wise Transition plan.

1 Declutter: Decluttering your space can help declutter our mind. Start one space at a time.

2 Get Outside: Enjoying nature helps reduce stress, increases endorphins, and lets you appreciate the world around you.

3 Bring the Outdors Inside: Plants can improve indoor air quality fresh air improves sleep. A dose of nature can enhance energy and performance.

4 Environmentally Friendly: Ditching unnecessary chemicals, unhealthy foods, unfriendly Earth practices, and bad habits/routines will improve health and improve the environment and ecosystem.

5 Know Your Preferred Environment: Know the environments that bring out the best in you and spend regular, quality time in them.

Summary: Don't underestimate the impact your environment has on you. Don't underestimate the need you have to be part of nature and don't underestimate the power you have in protecting the environment you engage with.

Our literal existence is entwined with the natural world, and the external world we build is based on the environments we create for ourselves and feel safe in. These are things to think about when you evaluate or aim to improve your environmental wellness.

Do you have a safe environment to recuperate in when the challenges of life start to have an effect on you? Do you know the best environments for you, those that invigorate you, increase your energy and bring you inner peace? Do you create an environment for yourself that is free from toxins so that it keep you healthy in body and mind?

Your environment is so much more than just the space you exist in or the surroundings you choose to engage with. It is a key factor in your external world, which is why it is such an important component for your overall wellness and wellbeing.

EXTERNAL DIMENSION: Social Wellness

Recap: Our social wellness focuses on how we connect with others, how we interact with others, and how we develop and maintain healthy relationships. Optimal social wellness also requires you to know when to distance yourself from those relationships that are no longer healthy for you.

Complete the assessment below to identify your current level of social wellness and fill in your 8Wise Map.

Social Wellness Evaluation

	Question	Rate yourself			
		Never	Rarely	Sometimes	Usually
1	I plan and spend enjoyable quality time with friends and family	1	2	3	4
2	I find opportunities to develop new relationships	1	2	3	4
3	I give priority to my own needs and feel comfortable saying 'no' to others	1	2	3	4
4	I feel supported and respected in my close relationships	1	2	3	4
5	I communicate effectively with others no matter the social interaction	1	2	3	4
6	I make efforts to improve the behaviours I know have caused upset to others	1	2	3	4
7	I seek out intimate relationships where values are shared, and mutual respect is demonstrated	1	2	3	4
8	I am respectful of others and appreciate the diversity of others	1	2	3	4
9	I have someone I can talk to about my most private thoughts and feelings	1	2	3	4
10	I give and take equally in cooperative relationships	1	2	3	4
Totals					
Total Score					/40

8Wise Map Score board

Using the total score for the assessment, find your score in row A of the table below, then identify your corresponding 8Wise plot number in row B.

Plot this number on your 8Wise Map to represent your score for this section

A	10	11 - 15	16 - 20	21 - 25	25 - 30	31 - 35	36 - 39	40
B	1	2	3	4	5	6	7	8

My Top 5 Social Wellness tips to consider when identifying your 8Wise Steps for your 8Wise Transition plan.

1 Reflection: Reflect on yourself and your social needs. What aspects of your social life do you enjoy? What parts would you like to improve?

2 Support System: Take time to identify who your support systems are, the people who you share a 50/50 relationship with.

3 Keep in Touch: Make time to keep in touch with the people in your support system. Keep those relationships strong.

4 Boundaries: Build healthy boundaries with people. Personal Boundaries are important because they set the basic guidelines of how you want to be treated.

5 Say Goodbye: Don't be scared of letting go of toxic people – how long someone has been in your life should not equate to how long you accept a negative relationship.

Summary: 'You are not an island' may be such a cliche, but it does not stop it from being the truth. As discussed, we are part of nature, we are animals and furthermore we are pack animals, so whether you like it or not, you crave human interaction. You need human interaction for your wellness and wellbeing, but for you to have optimal health and wellbeing that interaction needs to be as positive as possible. That doesn't mean that all social interactions have to be 'good' or 'great', it just means that we need to experience positives from as many interactions as possible, even the less helpful ones.

Everything plays a part: our communication, our self-esteem, our ability to disconnect a person from their behaviour *(people are not their behaviour and therefore should not be labelled as such)*, our ability to be assertive with people when it's necessary – and let's be honest, there will be a lot of times when it is necessary to be assertive. All of these elements play a part in helping us to develop robust social systems that are positive for our wellness and wellbeing.

Many of our challenging life events involve our social networks and so developing our social wellness is of paramount importance for our overall wellness and wellbeing.

LIFESTYLE DIMENSION: Occupational Wellness

Recap: Occupational wellness involves balancing work and leisure time, building relationships with co-workers, and managing workplace stress to develop a sense of satisfaction and achievement in relation to your job, your employer and your career. This includes finding work that maps to your values, interests and skills.

Complete the assessment below to identify your current level of occupational wellness and fill in your 8Wise Map.

Occupational Wellness Evaluation

	Question	Rate yourself			
		Never	Rarely	Sometimes	Usually
1	I balance work with all other areas of my life effectively	1	2	3	4
2	I get personal satisfaction and fulfilment from the work I do	1	2	3	4
3	I work for an organisation whose values match my own	1	2	3	4
4	I get an opportunity to use my strengths and skills daily	1	2	3	4
5	I effectively manage my work stress levels and responsibilities	1	2	3	4
6	I have the opportunity to contribute my skills, knowledge and talents to the wider organisation	1	2	3	4
7	I am developing the necessary skills and knowledge to move forward in my career	1	2	3	4
8	I know what I am looking for when seeking an employer and a new role	1	2	3	4
9	I take opportunities to learn new skills and develop	1	2	3	4
10	I strive to develop good work habits and effective working relationships	1	2	3	4
	Totals				
	Total Score				/40

8Wise Map Score board

Using the total score for the assessment, find your score in row A of the table below, then identify your corresponding 8Wise plot number in row B.

Plot this number on your 8Wise Map to represent your score for this section

A	10	11 - 15	16 - 20	21 - 25	25 - 30	31 - 35	36 - 39	40
B	1	2	3	4	5	6	7	8

My Top 5 Occupational Wellness tips to consider when identifying your 8Wise Steps for your 8Wise Transition plan.

1 Work-Life Balance: Do not focus too much of your time and energy on one area of your life. Instead, balance your time and energy across all areas.

2 Don't Settle: Stay motivated by continuing to set goals and work towards them, whether it is with your current employer, in your current role, or in your current career.

3 Develop: Find ways to increase knowledge and skills to keep you motivated, interested and stimulated.

4 Benefits: Identify and focus on the benefits to your current role and career. If your struggle to find any, then you need to make a change.

5 Say Goodbye: Don't be scared of letting go if you are unhappy. Look for something new and/or talk to a career counsellor if you feel stuck or unhappy.

Summary: As we established early on in this book, we are expected to spend most of our adult lives in work and so it is inevitable that our jobs and the concept of working or not working for a living can affect our mental health and wellbeing. It is not something I talk about in this book, but as I have a background in welfare to work, supporting the long-term unemployed back into employment. I have seen first-hand the effects unemployment can have on a person's mental health, and therefore, from my perspective, occupational wellness is relevant to those in work as well as those trying to find work.

Employment can cause us immense stress, and our occupational wellness has the ability to impact all seven of the remaining elements of wellness very quickly, so it is important to manage this area of wellness effectively. Employers are also starting to understand the long-term impact of poor occupational wellness of employees and its association with mental and physical health issues, which is why so many organisations are starting to bring wellness into the workplace through exciting initiatives. 8Wise is one of those initiatives that many organisations have chosen to use to offer support to their employees and improve the overall wellness and wellbeing of their workforce.

The key message for your occupational wellness is learning to manage the demands of your work with the demands of your personal life. It is an important balancing act to learn, but so is finding a job or an occupation that matches to your interests, skills, values, and preferred environment. It is important that your work brings you into contact with a suitable network and that it gives you a purpose every day that you can be proud of as this will boost your confidence and self-esteem. That's the beauty of the lifestyle dimension: it comes together with understanding yourself through your foundation, internal and external dimensions.

Make sure you look after your occupational wellness – look at your employment status, your work, job and career and really analyse them because if you don't have occupational wellness, then there is no doubt your entire wellness spectrum will be affected.

LIFESTYLE DIMENSION: Financial Wellness

Recap: Finances are such a common trigger for stress, and being able to minimise that worry and stress through feeling financially satisfied will enhance overall wellness and wellbeing.

Complete the assessment below to identify your current level of occupational wellness and fill in your 8Wise Map.

Financial Wellness Evaluation

	Question	Never	Rarely	Sometimes	Usually
		Rate yourself			
1	I understand what money means to me	1	2	3	4
2	I understand my incoming and outgoing finances	1	2	3	4
3	I live within my means	1	2	3	4
4	I access tools and information to help me manage my money effectively	1	2	3	4
5	I have a standard bank account that allows direct debits and standing orders	1	2	3	4
6	I have a savings account that pay into regularly	1	2	3	4
7	I manage my credit effectively and understand my credit score	1	2	3	4
8	I check my bank statements regularly to ensure there are no errors	1	2	3	4
9	I make my own financial responsibilities a priority before supporting or helping others with theirs	1	2	3	4
10	I understand financial language	1	2	3	4
Totals					
Total Score					/40

8Wise Map Score board

Using the total score for the assessment, find your score in row A of the table below, then identify your corresponding 8Wise plot number in row B.

Plot this number on your 8Wise Map to represent your score for this section

A	10	11 - 15	16 - 20	21 - 25	25 - 30	31 - 35	36 - 39	40
B	1	2	3	4	5	6	7	8

My Top 5 Financial Wellness tips to consider when identifying your 8Wise Steps for your 8Wise Transition plan.

1 Relationship With Money: Reflect on what money really means to you, and how it supports your values, beliefs, purpose and your overall wellbeing.

2 Financial Literacy: Take time to learn the language of money, have the knowledge and skills to make effective decisions and develop money management tools.

3 Financial Planning: Consider your current situation and then identify some clear goals and objectives for where you want your finances to be and why.

4 Money Managment: Track your monthly income and expenditure through a budget that is in a format of your choice and is user-friendly for you.

5 Say Goodbye to the Credit Cycle: Understand credit/debt cycle traps including the difficulties and process for getting out of debt as well as the difficulties associated with gaining, maintaining and re-gaining good credit.

Summary: To achieve genuine financial wellness, you have to first start by understanding what that really means to you because this provides you with the underpinning reason as to why financial issues trigger specific stresses for you. When you understand what it means to you, then you know how you need to manage to ensure your finances work for you in a way that does not affect your wellness and wellbeing.

Just like in any other aspect in your life, understanding the language of finance and developing some effective skills in managing your finances will help you remain financially in control or at least up-to-date with your financial situation which in itself can bring you some satisfaction.

Ultimately financial wellness provides us with an opportunity to live the life we want, and as long as your financial wellness is in sync with the other seven elements of your wellness spectrum, then you should have the balance required for optimal health and wellbeing. Money might not make the world go round but it definitely affects your world from both internal and external sources, so get up to speed with what your money means to you, what you want it to mean to you and how you want it to help you to establish the life and the lifestyle you want to achieve for your preferred levels of wellness and wellbeing.

The 8Wise Transition Plan

Now that you have your 8Wise Map ready and some tips to help you start to develop your 8Wise Milestones and Steps, it's time to start developing your 8Wise Transition plan. But this is just the first level of evaluation – to develop effective 8Wise Milestones and, more specifically, 8Wise Steps, you need to dig a little deeper.

I wouldn't leave you to do this alone – I am a therapeutic coach and psychotherapist, after all. I am like your mental wellness Wise Owl, here to guide you through your 8Wise Journey to improve your wellness and wellbeing and protect your mental health, and so we move onto the eight core steps of the 8Wise method.

It's time to do some real work, therapeutic coaching style – are you ready to get wise about your wellness and wellbeing with the 8Wise core eight coaching tools?

Chapter 12:

The 8Wise Ways

I want to jump in with this next bit by providing some clarity for you – 8Wise is not a one-size-fits-all approach. Now you might be thinking, 'What is this woman talking about, she has said throughout this book that anyone can use it, that it can work as both a recover and a prevention model, so how can it not be a one-size-fits-all approach?' And you are right, of course, I have said all of those things but … that still does not make it a one-size-fits-all approach. You see, how arrogant would I be to assume I know everything about everyone and so can create a one-size-fits-all approach? How arrogant would I be to assume I understood more about psychology and philosophy than those who have studied it and dedicated their entire lives to understanding every last detail of it? I want to assure you, I am not that arrogant!

So, to clarify:
Can everyone use 8Wise? Yes.
Can 8Wise benefit everyone? Yes.
Is 8Wise a one-size-fits-all approach? No.

Simply put … it's not one-size-fits-all because 8Wise is designed to be ANY size. It is a flexible approach that maps to you and your life. It's a framework that you use to create the activities you need to complete in your life that improve your wellness and wellbeing to protect your mental health. I'm not going to dictate to you what they should all be: that would give me control and power over your life and your mental health and that is not something I want to have – I want you to have that. I only want to have some form of control and power in my own life and support others to find theirs.

It is important to me that you create your own 8Wise Transition Plan for your own 8Wise Journey following the framework I have outlined in this book. You must adapt the plan to suit yourself and your life, so you can live a happier, healthier and more fulfilling life. This is the only way 8Wise will work for you. You will not benefit from following anyone else's 8Wise journey, just like they cannot benefit from following yours. This really is one of those moments where it is all about you, so don't hide from it, embrace it. Because I am not the answer, 8Wise is not the answer – you are the answer. 8Wise is the underpinning knowledge you now have, it is the framework you have to work to, and it is the support system you have to guide you, but you are ultimately the power source in this process. Are you ready for that?

I promised that this book would provide you with eight simple steps for a healthier and happier mind and I will deliver on that. Not only have I introduced you to the eight wellness elements of the 8Wise approach, but the remainder of this book includes eight core activities that I suggest you complete to help yourself to build an effective 8Wise Transition plan. The activities will help you to develop the

knowledge and confidence to make any life decisions moving forward regarding your wellness and wellbeing for a healthier and happier life. I use each of these activities with my clients and I am now sharing them with you; all you need to do is follow the instructions provided.

Wise Way One: Time Traveller

Resources: Pen, paper, quiet space, Time Traveller worksheet

Guidelines:

- Draw 3 columns: Column A – Positives, Column B – Negatives, Column C – Emotions.

- To start the activity, close your eyes and take a deep breath in through your nose, and then breathe out through your mouth.

- Repeat this two more times

- Let your mind start to wander and think about your current decade (for example ages, 0-10, 10-20, 20-30, 30-40, 40-50, 50-60, 60-70, 70-80, 80-90).

- In column A, write down your memories that were positive – aim for no more than five.

- In column B, write down your memories that were negative.

- In column C, write down your emotions about those memories (you can use the emotions wheel in activity five to help with this).

- Complete breathing activity again to end that mental time travel experience.

- When you are ready, repeat steps 4 through to 8 until you have time travelled through all decades in your life to date.

- When completed, assess your timeline:

  - What are the common themes?

  - Is there a pattern or common theme throughout the decades regarding your thinking, feeling and behaviours?

  - Was there a stand-out moment that you think may have triggered different things in your life?

  - Which 8Wise elements were affected by the life events?

  - What have you learned from seeing your life as one timeline?

Purpose of Exercise:

I once read a Chinese proverb that said, 'You don't know where you are going until you know where you have been.' I am a firm believer in this concept, because for me, the present can be full of confusion created by all the thoughts, feeling and behaviours of past events throughout your life. Your subconscious can be driving you through your life, but the specifics with regards to what is in your subconscious can be clouded, and so the only way to have a better understanding of your present is to go into your subconscious mind and bring the strongest memories into your conscious mind.

The strongest memories will most likely be those linked to high levels of emotion, whether that be positive or negative. Because as we discussed in earlier chapters, those that have stronger emotional connotations stay with us longer within the accessible parts of our subconscious mind. Those strong emotions can make it difficult to process those old experiences and draw a conclusion that frees ourselves from them and the impact they have on our wellness and wellbeing. But if we choose to review and evaluate the past whilst balancing our emotional and rational mindset to initiate our wise mindset, we are able to detach from those strong emotions, which will make processing the experiences easier and less traumatic. We are then able to make some decisions about how we might want to make changes for our future wellness and wellbeing in order to protect our longer-term metal and physical health.

TIMELINE EXERCISE Instructions:

The diagram below represents your personal timeline from birth to your current age.

Through reflection, in the table below list the memories you have for each decade of your own timeline.

0 to 10 years old		11 to 20 years old		21 to 30 years old		31 to 40 years old		50 plus	
Positives	Negatives	Positives	Negatives	Positives	Negatives	Positives	Negatives	Positives	Negatives

Wise Way Two: Minute by Minute

Resources: Pen, paper, calendar app or Daily Diary worksheet on page …

Guidelines:

- To start the activity, close your eyes and take a deep breath in through your nose, and then breathe out through your mouth.

- Repeat this two more times.

- Create a seven-day timetable: track your time and tasks for one week.

- Block out the time you wake up and go to sleep.

- Block out times you prepare and eat meals.

- Block out time for commuting and work.

- Block out time for hobbies/leisure/ relaxation/self-care.

- When completed, assess your timeline:

- Are you making time for everything?

- Does one thing dominate your time?

- Do you have wasted time?

- Are you making yourself a priority with sufficient 'me time' and self-care?

- Which 8Wise elements were affected by your time management?

Purpose of Exercise:

I believe wholeheartedly that my clients 'feel' and 'think' that they don't have enough time, and I also believe wholeheartedly that you may also feel and think the same. But I do not believe that time for self-care does not actually exist, because we control the time in our lives, and we choose what to spend it on. Yes, we have responsibilities, but effective time management ensures that you can fulfil those responsibilities and still have the required time left to make sure you are functioning at full capacity.

If you are not doing this, then one of those other things that you make a priority will eventually stop being done well, or at all, and that will then bring a new range of stressful situations and problems for you to manage. This can then lead to mental health issues – because if you don't care for yourself you cannot provide a good quality of care anywhere else, no matter what you tell yourself.

When we feel stressed and overwhelmed, those stressful emotions dominate our thinking, manifesting into every part of our day, leaving us feeling exhausted and frazzled. It is this process that leads us to feel we do not have any spare time when what we actually have is a stressed and frazzled mind that needs self-care in order to de-stress and un-frazzle so we can function more effectively and manage our time.

By completing this activity you will face the facts of your current time management and also life balance. You then have the ability to make clear decisions regarding the time you need to either increase or decrease on different activities and responsibilities for a more efficient, fulfilling and balanced life.

Sleep, nutrition, activity and relaxation should be your priority, followed by your responsibilities, if you want to protect your mental health.

Instructions:

Track your time and tasks for one week.

Block out the times for the following: wake up/hobbies/work/meals/relaxation/sleep

Time	MON	TUES	WED	THIRS	FRI	SAT	SUN
				MORNING			
06:30							
07:00							
07:30							
08:00							
08:30							
09:00							
09:30							
10:00							
10:30							
11:00							
11:30							
				AFTERNOON			
12:00							
12:30							
13:00							
13:30							
14:00							
14:30							
15:00							
15:30							
16:00							
16:30							

EVENING							
17:00							
17:30							
18:00							
18:30							
19:00							
19:30							
20:00							
20:30							

NIGHT							
21:00							
21:30							
22:00							
22:30							
23:00							
23:30							
00:00							

Review your week

1. Is use of time balanced?

2. What did you learn?

3. What could be improved?

Instructions:

Create a time management plan for one week, and follow it.

Block out: wake up/hobbies/work/meals/relaxation/sleep

Time	MON	TUES	WED	THIRS	FRI	SAT	SUN
				MORNING			
06:30							
07:00							
07:30							
08:00							
08:30							
09:00							
09:30							
10:00							
10:30							
11:00							
11:30							
				AFTERNOON			
12:00							
12:30							
13:00							
13:30							
14:00							
14:30							
15:00							
15:30							
16:00							
16:30							

EVENING							
17:00							
17:30							
18:00							
18:30							
19:00							
19:30							
20:00							
20:30							

NIGHT							
21:00							
21:30							
22:00							
22:30							
23:00							
23:30							
00:00							

Review your week

1. What went well?

2. What could be improved?

3. What did you learn?

Wise Way Three: The Inner Circle

Resources: Pen, Inner Circle worksheet

Guidelines:

- To start the activity, close your eyes and take a deep breath in through your nose, and then breathe out through your mouth.

- Repeat this two more times.

- Use the Inner Circle diagram at the end of the exercise.

- This diagram represents the relationships and support systems you have in your life. The circle in the centre represents you and the circles surrounding you are where your support systems are. If you place someone on the circles closest to your inner circle, you are claiming they are a strong support system for you. If you place someone in the circles further away from your inner circle, you are claiming that that they are a weaker support system for you.

- Think of the relationships of significance in your life, past and present, alive or deceased, and place them on the diagram in the circle you where you think they belong. Examples: parents, siblings, grandparents, guardians, friends, teachers, colleagues, managers, therapists, doctors, pets, religious elements etc.

- Think about who is a support to you? Who do you have a close bond to? Who is your support system?

- Examples of relationships: immediate family, wider family, friends, work colleagues, pets, religious symbols of importance (e.g. God), professional relationships (e.g. therapist, personal trainer), teacher, deceased people.

- When completed assess your timeline:

  - Who is closest and why?

  - Do you have enough interaction with those who are closest?

  - Do you want to bring anyone closer or move anyone further away?

  - Do you think everyone deserves to be on there?

  - Are there any toxic relationships you think need to end?

  - Which 8Wise elements are affected by your significant relationships and support system?

  - What have you learnt about your social networks and support system from this activity?

Purpose of Exercise:

I have said many times throughout this book that humans are pack animals and therefore we need a support system and crave a social network. But we also have to be realistic that the wrong social network or support system can bring us more problems and pain than we can actually manage, and so it is important to build the most effective and efficient support system for our mental health and wellbeing.

The relationships that bring us the most support do not have to be the same as anyone else's. They can come in different shapes and sizes, so try not to compare what you have to others – the key is having or developing the right support system for you.

I can say from personal experience that this activity was my most ground-breaking for my own 8Wise Journey. The truth hurt, but I never looked back, and I developed a support system that I now have pride in, who give me the confidence to be me – and you can too.

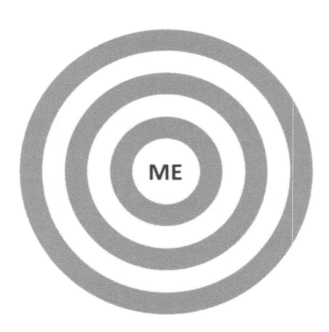

Wise Way Four: Your Daily Q&A

Resources: Pen, paper, 8Wise Journal or personal journal/diary

Guidelines:

- To start the activity, close your eyes and take a deep breath in through your nose, and then breathe out through your mouth.

- Repeat this two more times.

- Answer each of the following prompts into your chosen journal tool.

  1. What are the positives and negatives of the day?

  2. If you could do the day again what things that were in your control would you change?

  3. What emotions have dominated your day?

  4. What baggage from yesterday did you carry into today?

  5. What are you grateful for today?

  6. List two things you want to achieve tomorrow.

  7. List one thing you like about yourself.

  8. List one 8 Wise element you have focussed on today.

- When completed assess your answers:

    - How many of the issues today were out of your control?

    - Are there any questions you couldn't answer? Why?

    - Are stresses from previous days and weeks still dominating – if so, what can be done about them? (see problem solving tool on page ...)

    - Which of the 8Wise elements are affected by the events of the day?

- Complete breathing activity again to end the Q and A session.

Purpose of Exercise:

Reflecting on the day gives you some time and headspace to put it all into perspective before ending the day. It is important to be able to identify if any frustrations have been created through your own responses and behaviours (things you have control over), or the behaviours and actions of others (things that are out of your control).

It is very easy to become focused on the things that you have no control over, placing yourself within a hamster wheel of frustration and inner turmoil that you cannot get out of because you can't control the actions of others. It is more beneficial for your mental health that you learn to focus on the things you have control over and develop the skills to let go of the things that you cannot. It all starts with reflection.

It is also important to identify if any unresolved issues are affecting present situations or cognition, meaning thinking, feeling and behaviours. If they are then it's time to make an effort to resolve them through problem solving, leaving you free to only have to manage and respond to current events rather than a backlog too. If you don't deal with the backlog and carry it with you each day, then you have a high risk of developing dysfunctional stress, with the potential for it to develop into mental health issues.

Aim to end the day on a positive note. Focus on identifying the good in life and in yourself which will boost your self-esteem and confidence. This approach will help you to manage any issues that may have occurred throughout the day, but also those from the past and in the future too.

Wise Way Five: Emotional Analysis

Resources: Pen, paper, Emotions Wheel

Guidelines:

- This activity can be used with your daily Q & A or any time you feel emotional and need to reflect in order to manage your emotions and understand your response to things more effectively.

- To start the activity, close your eyes and take a deep breath in through your nose, and then breathe out through your mouth.

- Repeat this two more times.

- Using the Emotions Wheel diagram at the end of these instructions, identify your emotions:

  - First, start with choosing your primary emotion category (the one in the centre of the circle).

  - Staying within your emotion category, move to the secondary emotions in the second circle to narrow down the more precise feeling you are experiencing.

  - Move to the third circle to narrow it down further to the exact feeling.

- When you have identified your exact emotion, identify the life event or current issue that is triggering it.

- Use the problem-solving tool on page .... to find a solution to the problem triggering your emotions.

- Complete the breathing activity again to end the process.

Purpose of Exercise:

The basic rules of managing your emotions:

1. Identify the emotion
2. Sit and allow yourself to experience the emotion
3. Let the emotion go.

These are very fine rules, but I believe that to truly be free of that specific emotion, you sometimes need to manage it, take control of it and resolve the issue that triggered it, or it can become a 'boomerang emotion'. I use the term boomerang emotion to explain an emotion that you might be able to manage in the moment but, because it is linked to an ongoing problem or issue, it keeps coming back only to get stronger and stronger the longer it stays.

I was guilty of this cycle for many years, claiming to be too busy to actually put the time and effort into resolving the issue. By not resolving it, the emotions can get so strong they can lead to behavioural and mental health reactions such as procrastination, fear, anxiety, panic and even depression, so don't welcome in the boomerang emotion – learn to manage those emotions by balancing them, and then resolving the trigger issues.

To manage your emotions, you need to balance out your emotional mindset with your logical or rational mindset in order to utilise your wise mindset effectively. This requires you to use the skills linked to rational thinking such as analysis, assessment and problem solving. You need to start this process by assessing and analysing your emotions accurately, hence the narrowing-down process of this exercise.

Emotions are nothing to be scared of – they are to be understood with open eyes because they are telling you something. They are communicating to you that something is not right, triggering something inside of you that cannot and should not be ignored, but instead should be understood as part of the process for improving your wellness and wellbeing and protecting your mental health.

The Emotions Wheel

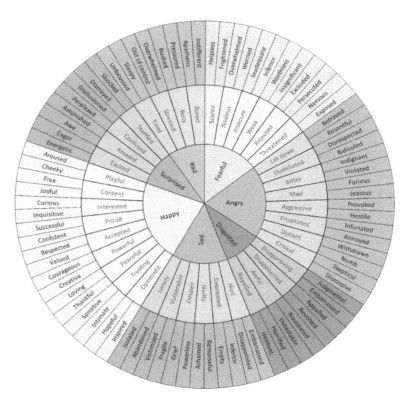

Wise Way Six: Values

Resources: Pen, paper, Values Worksheet

Guidelines:

- To start the activity, close your eyes and take a deep breath in through your nose, and then breathe out through your mouth.

- Repeat this two more times.

- Listed after these instructions are 50 values. Read through the list and when you find a value that describes you, circle it.

- Next, reduce your list so you have no more than ten core values that you strongly connect with, and rank them in order of importance.

- Reflect on the meaning of each of the ten, and identify how you demonstrate that value in your daily life.

- Repeat the exercise, focussing only on values you do not agree with and narrow it down again to no more than ten core 'anti-values'.

- Reflect on how others may demonstrate both your values and anti-values, reflect on how it made you feel and behave towards them.

- Complete the breathing activity again to end the process.

Purpose of Exercise:

Who are you? By that, I mean who are you at your core, because that is what really matters when it comes to your mental health.

When we are able to identify who we are via our core values and, most importantly, accept who we are, we are then in a better state of mind for our self-esteem and confidence, which has a knock-on effect to our full spectrum of wellness.

It is equally important to understand the values or 'anti-values', as I like to call them, that do not 'sit right' with us, as this helps us to understand why we might respond to different situations, behaviours, and in some cases people the way we do. If their value base does not align with ours, it will cause a negative reaction, whether it is conscious or subconscious. This can apply to employers too and may explain why sometimes you just never feel right working for some employers.

I remember doing this exact same exercise during my own 'recovery' process, because getting to know and understand myself was probably the most fundamental important part of the process – after all, how can I make decisions for myself if I don't know who I am? How can I live a life that is authentic to me and how can I ever have confidence in the life I have created? I now live by the values I identified, and I have more confidence making decisions that are right for me because I know that if it aligns with my values, it is something I can live with. I also learnt what money means to me because money had been a huge cause of stress throughout my life. What I learnt was that money, for me, means security. If I saved money, it was to feel secure, and if I spent money it was because I was feeling insecure. As I learnt this about myself, I was able to manage my money more realistically, and that in itself decreased a lot of my stress.

'Who am I?' – three little words put together to make a question that when actually answered can provide you with stability, self-esteem, confidence, resilience and a pride in who you are and what your purpose is in life.

Identifying my own value base genuinely became the benchmark for my recovery, as it has for many of my clients too, and I have no doubt it will play an important role in your 8Wise journey too.

Values Clarification

Identify your values and anti-values from those listed in the table below.

- **ACCEPTANCE** To be accepted as I am
- **ACCURACY** To be correct in my opinions and actions
- **ACHIEVEMENT** To accomplish and achieve
- **ADVENTURE** To have new and exciting experiences
- **ATTRACTIVENESS** To be physically attractive
- **AUTHORITY** To be in charge of others
- **AUTONOMY** To be self-determining and independent
- **BEAUTY** To appreciate beauty around us
- **CARING** To take care of others
- **COMFORT** To have a pleasant, enjoyable life
- **COMMITMENT** To make a long-lasting and deep commitment to another person

- **COMPASSION** To feel and show concern for others
- **COMPLEXITY** To have a life full of variety and change
- **CONTRIBUTION** To make a contribution that will last after I am gone
- **COURTESY** To be polite and considerate to others
- **CREATIVITY** To have new and original ideas
- **DEPENDABILITY** To be reliable and trustworthy
- **DUTY** To carry out my duties and responsibilities
- **ECOLOGY** To live in harmony with and protect the environment
- **FAME** To be known and recognized

- **FAMILY** To have a happy, loving family
- **FLEXIBILITY** To adjust to new or unusual situations easily
- **FORGIVENESS** To be forgiving of others
- **FRIENDS** To have close, supportive friends
- **FUN** To play and have fun
- **GENEROSITY** To give what I have to others
- **GENUINENESS** To behave in a manner that is true to who I am
- **GOD'S WILL** To seek and obey the will of God
- **GROWTH** To keep changing and growing

- **HEALTH** To be physically well and healthy
- **HELPFULNESS** To be helpful to others
- **HONESTY** To be truthful and genuine
- **HUMILITY** To be modest and unassuming
- **HUMOR** To see the humorous side of myself and the world
- **INDEPENDENCE** To be free from depending on others
- **INDUSTRY** To work hard and well at my life tasks
- **INNER PEACE** To experience personal peace
- **INTIMACY** To share my innermost experience with others

- **JUSTCE** To promote equal and fair treatment for all
- **KNOWLEDGE** To learn and possess valuable knowledge
- **LEISURE** To make time to relax and enjoy
- **LOGIC** To live rationally and sensibly
- **LOVED** To be loved by those close to me
- **LOVING** To give love to others
- **MASTERY** To be competent in my everyday activities
- **MODERATION** To avoid excess and find a middle ground
- **MONOGAMY** To have one close, loving relationship

- **ORDERLINESS** To have a life that is well-ordered and organized
- **PLEASURE** To have experiences that feel good
- **POPULARITY** To be well-liked by many people
- **POWER** To have control over others
- **PURPOSE** To have meaning and direction in life
- **REALISM** To see and act realistically and practically
- **RESPONSIBILITY** To make and carry out important decisions
- **RISK** To take risks and chances
- **ROMANCE** To have intense, exciting love in my life

- **SAFETY** To be safe and secure
- **SELF-ACCEPTANCE** To like myself as I am
- **SELF-CONTROL** To be self-disciplined and govern my own activities
- **SELF-CONTROL** To be self-disciplined and govern my own activities
- **SELF-ESTEEM** To feel positive about myself
- **SELF-KNOWLEDGE** To have a deep, honest understanding of myself
- **SERVICE** To be of service to others
- **SEXUALITY** To have an active and satisfying sex life
- **SIMPLICITY** To live life simply, with minimal needs

- **SELF-KNOWLEDGE** To have a deep, honest understanding of myself
- **SERVICE** To be of service to others
- **SEXUALITY** To have an active and satisfying sex life
- **SIMPLICITY** To live life simply, with minimal needs
- **SPIRITUALITY** To grow spiritually
- **STABILITY** To have a life that stays fairly consistent
- **STRENGTH** To be physically strong
- **TOLERANCE** To accept and respect those different from me
- **VIRTURE** To live a morally pure and excellent life
- **WEALTH** To have plenty of money

Wise Way Seven: My Value-Based CV

Resources: Pen, paper, quiet space

Guidelines:

- This activity builds from the previous value-based activity

- To start the activity, close your eyes and take a deep breath in through your nose, and then breathe out through your mouth.

- Repeat this two more times.

- Curriculum Vitae is a Latin expression, loosely translated to mean 'the course of my life'. For this activity, you use it for value-based achievements and not career and academic ones.

- Use the table at the end of these instructions to develop your value-based CV.

- When the activity is finished, complete the breathing activity again to end the process.

Purpose of Exercise:

The amount of times I have changed and developed my CV (or as my American friends call it, my resume) is ridiculous. It's a two-page document that outlines what I have done in my career to attract potential employers, but it's not the story of who I am, or my life in detail. Don't get me wrong, it did me wonders in my career, but I placed so much emphasis on it, as if that information was what defined me. What I later learnt about myself is that it is great to be good at business and organisational strategy, but for me it is not as great an achievement as having the ability to be empathetic to both others and myself, because that is an important factor in my core value base.

What I realised during my own recovery, along with the fact I did not really know myself, is that because I did not know myself I was placing too much value and importance on my worth to others – how I could impress others. As my career was 'my thing' and hiking up the corporate ladder was 'my goal', my CV became my badge of honour. Sadly, having a gleaming CV did not give me the self-esteem I was clearly lacking; in fact, it provided me with the exact opposite, because I never really felt worthy or good enough for my achievements. This is because they were external-world-orientated and did not connect with my inner word at all. Meaning they were tick boxes, things I did because I thought that is what others and wider society expected from me. They did not link to my own values, because at that stage I was hiding from who I really was.

Please don't misunderstand: I am very proud of my career achievements, but it became more important for me, my mental health and wellbeing to become proud of myself as a person, and more importantly to like myself as a person. So, I took my favourite document and turned it on its head to create 'Your Values-Based CV', a document that shows character achievements rather than just academic and career-based ones.

This exercise is not an easy one – it forces you to dig deep and really look at your values from the perspective of how you manifest them into your life through actions and behaviours, so you are living a life of true authenticity. It asks you to prove it through past experiences – not for me, your family, friends, employers, colleagues etc., but for yourself, so not only can you answer the question 'Who am I?', but you can also answer it with true conviction, rather than lip service.

Being at one with yourself is the most powerful thing you can achieve in your personal development. It gives you a baseline to map everything in life to, which in turn gives you a framework for navigating your life effectively.

---

1. Personal Profile – Who am I? What are my core values? What are my core beliefs?

Top Tip: These are big questions – so to help with this, think about things that upset you in real life, world events, political events, social events, news articles, things you see on social media, situations you have experienced. When you have a list of what they are, think about what upsets you about them – the answer to those questions will start to highlight your values and beliefs. When we dislike or get upset about something, it is usually because it goes against our core values and beliefs.

2. Values Experience – When did my core values develop? Where did my values develop? Who influenced my values?

Top Tip: We are not born with values; we are influenced by external factors such as our parents, our guardians, adults of significance, relationships of significance, our culture, our friends, our community, situations that happened to us, situations that we observed, books we have read, religious beliefs, etc. Think about each of your values and beliefs, when they developed, who influenced them, how they developed.

3. Skills & Competencies – What skills have I developed due to my values? What competencies have been developed due to my values?

Top Tip: Most of us are not born with a specific skill set; we develop them over time, usually in response to situations or focussed learning. Think about skills you have developed due to experiences you had, or interests linked to your values and beliefs. An example of this may be music, yoga, exercise, nutrition, empathy, listening skills, patience, ambition, drive, disconnection, education. These skills and competencies may be negative or positive in your life; all are important to understanding who you are and why.

4. Achievements – What have I achieved in life due to my values and beliefs? When have my values and beliefs held me back or stopped me achieving something?

Top Tip: We are led by our values and beliefs even when we think we are not. What successes and positive experiences have you had that are an outcome of your values and beliefs?

Equally important are what failures or negative experiences have been an outcome of your values and beliefs.

5. Aspirations – What do I want to achieve? What do I hope to achieve and how will my values and beliefs support this?

Top Tip: Think of what you want to achieve and how you can use your values and beliefs to do this. This may also include how you may need to adapt your values and beliefs if they are holding you back.

6. References – Who has benefitted from my value base? Who would validate my value base?

Top Tip: Who has experienced your values and beliefs through situations with you? This could be relationships you have strengthened, people you have helped, people you have refused to help, people you have distanced yourself from, positive situations, negative situations.

Wise Way Eight: 8Wise Transition Plan

Resources: Pen, paper or 8Wise Journal, quiet space, 8Wise Transition Plan template

Guidelines:

- To start the activity, close your eyes and take a deep breath in through your nose, and then breathe out through your mouth.

- Repeat this two more times.

- Use the information you have learnt about yourself in the seven previous activities along with the findings from your 8Wise Map to create an effective personal 8Wise Transition Plan.

- Plan to review the 8Wise Transition Plan every twelve weeks, making sure that all steps and milestones align with your value base, your life responsibilities and daily schedule.

- Use values to identify and understand why you might experience problems in relationships with friends, family, colleagues and employers, and find solutions rather than staying fixed in an unhealthy situation.

- Use the emotions tracker to understand exactly what you are feeling and why you are feeling it and allow yourself to experience that feeling – do not supress it. Then use the problem-solving tool to proactively find solutions to the issues that trigger those emotional responses.

- These eight exercises provide you with a foundation of information that will help you with your 8Wise Journey.

Purpose of Exercise:

The aim of all of these exercises is to help you start reflecting and developing an accurate account of the reality of your life, who you are and how you feel, as well as providing you with some tools to help you navigate through the life events that trigger the responses that can lead to mental health issues.

Through this personal development you start to change and adapt your conditioned mindset. This is a crucial component in stress management and improved wellness and wellbeing. It is your conditioned mindset that determines how you respond to the external factors in your life that trigger your stress levels and impact your eight areas of wellness as outlined in the 8Wise model. Therefore, to be able to have a healthy conditioned mind which transitions into improved wellness and wellbeing, you need to:

1. Know and understand your life journey to date – this is your unique path that has led you to where you are right now.

2. Know who you are and what you believe in, so you are able to understand what you respond well to and what you respond less well to, in order to manage future events in a healthier way.

3. Take accountability and be realistic about your life and the choices you have made and continue to make.

Make changes where needed and accept where you have control and where you don't.

4. Give yourself permission and time to identify, accept and maybe experience your emotions rather than supress them, otherwise they may come back bigger, bolder and more damaging.

5. Understand your 8Wise wellness dimensions: Foundation, Internal, External and Lifestyle, and implement life strategies that boost them and have a positive impact on your eight wellness elements.

6. Make your whole self a priority, not just specific elements of your life

7. Never be too scared or too proud to ask for help, whether that be from professionals, friends, family or colleagues. We are not born to live this life alone, or manage alone, so reach out and accept the support of those who reach back

8. Let your 8Wise journey lead you to a happier, healthier and more fulfilling life. Let it help you to protect your longer-term mental and physical health through improved wellness and wellbeing, because the truth is this life you are living right now is not forever, so make the most of it. Make sure you create the memories and experiences that fill you with joy, move forward from the events that have held you back in the past, and most importantly, like and love yourself – your mental health will thank you for it.

Over the next few pages are some additional tools that can help you with all elements of your 8Wise Journey. They can be used alongside all of the activities listed, as well as any you may create for yourself as part of the self-reflection strategy you might implement for your new 8Wise wellness and wellbeing routine.

No matter where you are with your current mental health, whether you be in recovery, maintenance or prevention mode, I wish you well with your 8Wise Journey. It has helped me, and many of my clients, and I believe it saved my life, so I am confident it can be a great support to you too.

Most importantly, I wish you well in achieving your goal of improving your wellness and wellbeing to protect your longer-term mental and physical health for a happier, healthier and more fulfilling life.

8 Wise™ Transition Plan

Name:

Date:

Aim	Score	8W Steps		Measurable	Budget	Resource	Deadline	Achieved
Emotional Wellness	/ 8	1.						
		2.						
		3.						
Physical Wellness	/ 8	1.						
		2.						
		3.						
Spiritual Wellness	/ 8	1.						
		2.						
		3.						
Intellectual Wellness	/ 8	1.						
		2.						
		3.						

8W Milestone 1: 12 weeks

8W Milestone 2: 6 months

8W Milestone 3: 12 months

8 WISE WELLNESS PROGRAMME

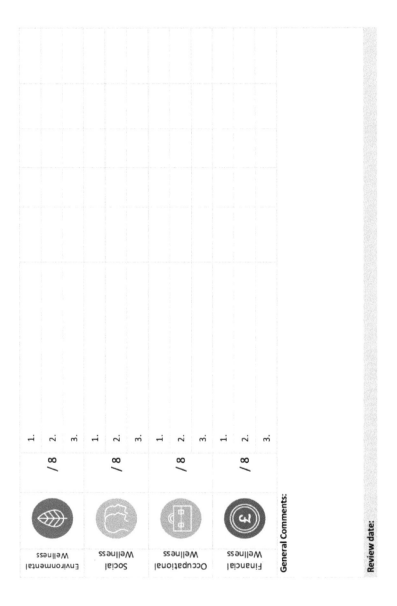

		1.
Environmental Wellness	/ 8	2.
		3.
Social Wellness	/ 8	1.
		2.
		3.
Occupational Wellness	/ 8	1.
		2.
		3.
Financial Wellness	/ 8	1.
		2.
		3.

General Comments:

Review date:

Chapter 13:

Drawing to a Close

We are drawing to a close on this adventure together, and I am leaving your 8Wise Journey firmly in your hands with the knowledge and belief that it has helped many people before you, providing them with a framework, tool, model and a method to manage the challenges and transitions that life will always throw at them, and it can help you too.

The only guarantee we have in life is that the journey towards our final destination is never going to be smooth – there will always be bumps in the road, and waves to ride that are bigger and stronger than any we have experienced before. But we can problem solve those challenges, we can overcome those challenges, and we can move forward from those challenges. I know first-hand that it doesn't always feel like this, that sometimes we can feel lost, alone, scared, beaten, exhausted by it all, and that is why I created 8Wise. I wanted to develop a tool that could help and support with gaining clarity about who you are and what you can achieve. I wanted to help you develop the strength to fight your fears and make positive life-changing decisions for you and for your health. I wanted to help you improve your wellness and wellbeing so you are in a position to reach a state of mental health that can positively impact your physical health too.

8Wise was created as part of my own recovery process, and it was then tried and tested on a wide range of private clients during one-to-one therapeutic coaching sessions. The therapeutic coaching approach combines therapeutic methodology with coaching methodology for an end-to-end holistic approach for the client.

The common theme amongst all clients is that what they present to me as their 'issue' is often the surface issue, and so it is through investigative work we identify the core issues, those that are more deep rooted within the unconscious and subconscious mind. We use the 8Wise Map and a range of the exercises, many of which are shared with you in this book, to piece together the true picture, the depth of the issue and those important triggers, so we can then develop a personalised 8Wise Transition plan with milestones and steps to move forward.

Even though peoples' experiences are all very different due to the lives they have led, the one common factor amongst them all is that they leave the 8Wise programme with a better understanding of who they are and what makes them tick, and that is where the confidence to follow through with their plan comes from.

I have worked with many clients and I was debating with myself as to whether I should provide case studies to prove to you how 8Wise works. But, to be honest, my decision was that all my clients deserve their privacy with regards to their 8Wise

Journey. But I will give you an overview of the types of issues that have been resolved.

> *Anxiety, bereavement, bullying, burnout, business issues, career changes, confidence, dating, divorce, depression, domestic violence, emotional abuse, empty nesting, family issues, grief, life challenges, life transitions, panic attacks, phobias, parenting, promotions, public speaking, stress, self-esteem, self-harm, sexual abuse, sexuality, transgender, menopause, relocation, relationship issues, renovations, workplace stress and work life/balance.*

I would like to take this opportunity to say thank you to every client who has trusted me with their story – it's always a privilege to be part of their 8Wise Journey and to be trusted with their life experiences to date.

Although for confidentiality reasons, I don't want to share clients' stories with you, I think two specific ones will be very useful for you. I have changed the names and some of the specific details to protect the individual's identities.

So here is the first. I remember my first call with Jane – she was a straight talker who liked organisation, practicality and to always stay in control. We had already sent a few emails back and forth so she could check me out and make sure I was not 'fluffy', as she told me she was looking for a 'no bollocks' therapist – luckily for me, I guess that's what I am.

Her reason for coming to me was she was unhappy in life and had bouts of low mood and depression that she was open and honest about with her friends. She was successful, a career woman at the top of her game, but she had been feeling this way since successfully combatting and beating a life-threatening illness.

The 'no bollocks' promise I made to her led to a rewarding process, as she committed fully to the 8Wise Journey in her own 'no bollocks' fashion.

Jane wanted to feel happy again, feel like she was living life again, and the safe life she was living was preventing her from achieving this. We started to shake things up where her life most needed shaking up – her occupational wellness and more specifically her work-life balance. Jane worked a 16-hour day, and so we first started working on a new schedule that reduced the work hours and increased the hours for fun and wellbeing, which included self-care. This helped to improve her physical wellness because part of her self-care was to get more active, start riding her horses again and eat more nutritionally rather than living on chocolate. Alongside all of this came a better sleep routine and more importantly, better sleep quality.

When we had a good level of physical wellness in place, we then moved onto her emotional wellness and started to face head on some of those deep-rooted emotions she had been storing away for some time, as most of us do, as well as those that had developed due to her illness. By working through each of the eight elements one by one, task by task, Jane's mood started to lift, she started to make decisions about changes she wanted to make. She started to accept the importance of wellness and wellbeing to balance out work and she began to feel optimistic and motivated about what she wanted to do in her life.

By the time Jane's 8Wise programme with me came to an end, we had tackled the depression, faced head on some of the emotions, blockers and thoughts that had been holding her back from living a fulfilling life, and talked through the decisions she chose to make for her life moving forward. She made plans for her career and gained a sense of clarity about it all, which she said was for the first time in five years, and I had no doubt that was true. She told me, 'I know longer feel like a zombie in my own life.' She had implemented strategies to improve her emotional wellness through committing to techniques that she could use to reflect with, and she had implemented an excellent self-care strategy that included the guilt-free notion of some days off to 'just chill'.

Jane started to realign with her values and beliefs and feel proud of them, and wanting to live a life by them. She started to acknowledge the importance of the environment she lived in and quickly understood that changes needed to be made to encourage her to engage with the real world, the outside world rather than just the office.

She started to reconnect with old friends and colleagues, and she made some big decisions regarding her career and her future finances. She fully committed to her 8Wise Journey and changed her views on how she wanted to live her life, or as much as a global pandemic and lockdown would allow her to (this was during the time that Covid-19 was affecting life in the UK).

We ended our sessions with a plan to work together at each 8Wise review stage, every twelve weeks. Unfortunately, we never got an opportunity to work together again. During the early stages of writing this book, Jane received the news that the original life-threatening condition she had experienced had returned and was now terminal, and as I write these last few pages, Jane has sadly since passed away, peacefully.

Why would this tragedy, a young woman in the prime of her life passing away, be the client I am most proud of working with? It was simply because she was a 'no bollocks' person. Someone who accepted that she was unhappy, and that it was her place to change it. She was someone who made the decision to not only start the process but fully commit to it with one intention only: to improve her wellness and wellbeing, have a better quality of life and smile again. We could all do with a little bit of the grit Jane showed at some stage in our lives; she was a force to be reckoned with, a gorgeous, smart, funny, intelligent woman and it was a true pleasure to work with her.

After her passing, I received a message from a friend that simply said, 'Thank you for the work you did with her – I know she was feeling better about herself as a result of it, so it was very worthwhile.' This made me feel very proud, not because of the work 'I' did, because with all clients, it is never me who does the work, it is always them. For Jane, I simply provided her with a tool, a framework to do the work herself. As I type this with tears falling down my cheeks, I am proud, proud to have worked with her, proud to have learnt from her, proud to have supported her and proud to have played a part in her gaining a better quality of life in what became her final months.

I am proud that her journey has now become part of my own journey and her story can now inspire so many more to focus on getting a better quality of life for themselves too. Because ultimately that is what 8Wise is really all about, a tool with some simple steps that can help you achieve a better quality of life from this moment onwards, and isn't that what we all deserve to have? The best quality of life possible whilst we are here?

If you choose to commit to 8Wise and by doing so commit to the process of making your own wellness and wellbeing an important factor in your life, just like Jane did, you can improve your quality of life and maybe the quality of life of those around you too.

I don't want to leave you here just yet. I have one last 8Wise Journey to share with you – my own.

My story is now documented throughout this book, but to clarify some core points:

- I had been a close spectator of mental health issues – anxiety, clinical depression and nervous breakdown – from age eight.

- I had seen inside my first mental health hospital as a visitor aged ten, and then again aged eighteen.

- I understood about suicide and its aftermath when I was sixteen.

- I supressed all thoughts, feelings and memories from my childhood until I was thirty-eight.

- I learned through therapy that I had been experiencing depression for over twenty years, completely undiagnosed.

- By the time this book is published, my life will have been entangled both as a spectator and participant with mental health issues in one way or another for almost forty years.

I once felt shame about all of that, but I no longer feel shame – I am proud of my battle scars, the journey I have had so far and the people I have met along the way. I am proud that through my own mental health experience I developed 8Wise as a tool to help others take care of their own long-term mental and physical health through improved wellness and wellbeing.

This is my 8Wise Journey:

I scored low against all eight elements and so I really was looking at the process as a blank canvass, drawing a line in the sand and committing to making a better future.

Emotional Wellness: I was suffering with extremely low self-esteem and negative self-talk. The dialogue in my head was outright bullying towards myself. As I always say, these harsh words we use on ourselves never start as our own words; they usually start as someone else's, and I started to acknowledge that my own opinion of myself had been developed from the bullying I had received at different stages in my life, a common story for so many of us.

True Story: I put off writing this book because I once told a friend I wanted to write a book and they said to me, 'Great idea, but please don't write one of those self-help books or "story of my sad life" books because they are so pathetic.' I obviously took that to mean I was pathetic, and everyone else would see that if I wrote the book I wanted to write. So I put it off, until I realised that was their opinion, nothing else, and that many people could benefit from my book and that my story is not sad – it's powerful, authentic and it's my truth and that does not make me pathetic, it makes me human. Funnily enough, that person now writes for a UK-based soap opera, which is basically writing stories about fake sad lives.

Physical Wellness: This has always been one of my harder elements to tackle. I am an emotional eater, a binge eater, an overeater and have a tendency for insomnia when experiencing high levels of stress – this, of course, effects my health in general, which is why it has become my most important element to conquer. It has been an uphill battle and I have fallen many times, but I keep pushing forward with it, making small steps each time. I now do yoga, eat nutritionally, keep up-to-date with my health checks (something I never did out of fear and sheer health anxiety) and I sleep, which is the biggest outcome of them all.

Spiritual Wellness: I really did not know myself – I thought I did, but I was just blending in as much as I could to try and feel like I fit in, which I never achieved. I aligned myself to whatever group of friends I was with to feel safe and comfortable and this had caused a great imbalance for me because I had no core belief system or value base. I worked a lot on this and through that process started to create a new inner dialogue, kicking all of those past bullies back to where they belong – the wilderness. I know who I am, what I can achieve and most importantly, what I want to achieve and stand for in this life – this process gave me purpose, and completely redirected my life.

Intellectual Wellness: I was so bored; I had fallen into my career and made a success of it, but I was not fulfilled to the levels I needed to be feel intellectually stimulated. I decided to retrain and move back towards a career I had planned for over a decade before – therapy. For three years, I retrained and found my intellectual stimulation again, much to the annoyance of my husband at times no doubt, because I would not shut up about it and started to read all people and all situations. Even to this day, people assume I am analysing anyone I meet. A friend was recently introducing his new girlfriend to us and she let it slip that he had warned her I would analyse her. For the record, I have not – well maybe just a little, but it is something I actively try not to do, unless it is required as part of my job, or as part of my people-watching hobby when sat alone in coffee shops watching the world around me.

Environmental Wellness: Through my therapeutic process, I identified that security and stability were of extreme importance to me, as previously mentioned, but it is something that my husband and I both have in common. When we really started to reflect on our life, we identified that we were not in the most suitable environment for us and so we made the decision to change, and back to Liverpool we moved. It was a wise decision, and we have both flourished as a result of it.

Social Wellness: This was another big one for me. I am an introvert and the close friends I did have lived all across the country and I never got to see them as often as I liked, and most importantly, as often as I needed to. So I felt isolated and lonely. When I got to Liverpool, I actively pushed myself out of my comfort zone and established new relationships and new friendships, many of whom I believe will become life-long friends.

I also let some friendships go along the way. I remember reading Jim Carey once saying, 'If you leave my life, it is not that I don't want you to eat, I just don't want you to eat at my table,' and that's how I feel about the people who have passed through my life. I am grateful for every one of them for the role they have played and wish them all well, but to keep hold of a toxic relationship that causes me pain or affects my mental health is no longer acceptable for my long-term wellness and wellbeing journey; I care for myself much more that that now.

Occupational Wellness: This was the big change in my life, because I was miserable. I was not satisfied by my achievements or what I did day-to-day, so it had to change. I decided to pool all my skills together, say goodbye to my safe and secure career in senior management in the corporate world and set up my own business. Dalton Wise Coaching and Therapy: supporting people with mental health and wellness through one-to-one therapeutic service, group workshops and consultancy to organisations to help with wellbeing in the workplace.

I have been fortunate enough to work with clients all over the world, which boosted my confidence enough to finally write this book. I had to stretch my comfort zone, align myself with my skills and lean on my self-esteem to finally get here, and as of today, writing this, I can confirm I am fulfilled in my career and have a true purpose in what I am trying to achieve with it, and at the same time ticking off a bucket list item too, with this book.

Financial Wellness: What I learnt was that I needed stability and security in my life for finances not to have a negative impact on me. We develop so many of our thoughts, feelings and connections to money from watching the experiences of our parents and I had to let some of that go. In my thirties, money equated to success, so by having money I was hoping that it would boost my self-esteem. This did not happen. Through reflection I learned to understand what finances really mean to me and developed a healthier relationship with money. These days it has very little to do with how much I have or do not have; for me, it's about understanding that my income does not define me, it does not make me a success, it does not automatically lead to safety and security, it simply helps me to live the lifestyle I want to live, and that has been a very freeing realisation during my 8Wise Journey.

I worked with a counsellor for over a year to help me work through my personal 8Wise Journey and with a clinical psychologist for over two years to help me develop the skills to become a good therapist. I still work with them to this day, to keep me on track, providing the best possible service to my clients.

Investing in this has been the best money I ever spent, because I realised that sometimes I just need a helping hand to guide me along the path, to get me out of my own head and live effectively between my internal and external world. Having someone who won't judge me, someone who won't interfere or try to sway my thoughts or beliefs but will simply walk beside me with empathy has been priceless.

I can't be that for everyone, no matter how much I would like to, but I hope that my 8Wise model helps you in that way a little.

I talked a lot about the 'one in four' and the 'other three' earlier in this book and I wanted to clarify a very important point – there is no shame in being part of that statistic, no matter which part you feel you may be. That statistic represents the reality of humans and life in this modern world, and so just know that wherever you may be within that statistic you can be the other side of it at any time too.

I created 8Wise to help you to manage that potential turbulence so that you can continue to work towards a state of optimal mental health. It helped me, it has helped my clients, and I firmly believe that it can help you too. So, I wish you well with your 8Wise Journey and I hope it can bring you balance in your life and a sense of confidence that no matter what life throws at you, you can overcome it because you have the tools to do so.

So, get wise about your wellness and wellbeing with 8Wise and protect your longer-term mental and physical health for a happier, healthier and more fulfilling life – that, my friends, is the 8Wise way and I wish you well with it.

Afterword

The 'One in Four' or the 'Other Three'

Why does any of this matter? Why is everyone starting to talk about mental health? Why do I care about mental health? Why should you care about mental health?

To start with, the statistics are scary.

All statistics below are from 2020

According to the Institute for Health Metrics Evaluation, 971 million people of the global population are suffering with their mental health.

In the UK, it is commonly acknowledged that one in four people will experience a mental health problem in any given year *(Mental Health Org)* and across the pond 46% of Americans will meet the criteria for a diagnosable mental health condition sometime in their life. *(Mental Health America)*

Mental Health America provided a further breakdown of statistics based on specific mental health conditions and their prevalence rates (the proportion of people in a population who have a particular disease or attribute at a specified point in time or over a specified period of time) and this is what they published:

Overall

- Number of US adults with mental illness: 44 million
- Percent of US adults with mental illness: 18%

Anxiety

- Lifetime prevalence of any anxiety disorder: 31.6%
- Number of US adults with anxiety disorders: 42.5 million
- Anxiety disorders are among the most common mental illnesses in America

Addiction/Substance Use Disorder

- Percent of US adults with a substance use disorder in the past year: 8%
- Number of US adults with a substance use disorder in the past year: 19 million
- Percent of youths aged 12 to 17 with a substance use disorder in the past year: 4.6%
- Number of youth with a substance use disorder in the past year: 1.1 million

Bipolar Disorder

- Past year prevalence of bipolar disorder: 1.8%
- Number of US adults with bipolar disorder: 3.3 million
- An estimated 2.5% of US adults experience bipolar disorder at some time in their lives.

Depression

- Percent of US adults with major depression: 7.1%
- Number of US adults with depression: 17.3 million
- Percent of youth (aged 12-17) with major depression: 13%
- Number of youth (aged 12-17) with major depression: 3.1 million
- Percent of youth with severe depression: 9%
- Number of youth (aged 12-17) with severe depression: 2 million
- Major depression is one of the most common mental illnesses

Post-Traumatic Stress Disorder (PTSD)

- Percent of people (age 13+) in US with PTSD (lifetime prevalence): 5.7%
- Percent of people (age 13+) in US with PTSD (one year prevalence): 3.7%
- Number of US adults with PTSD: 12 million

Schizophrenia

- Percent of US adults with schizophrenia: <1%
- Number of US adults with schizophrenia: 1.5 million

Suicidal Thoughts

- Percent of US adults with suicidal thoughts: 4% per year
- Number of US adults with suicidal thoughts: 9.8 million

Once upon a time, I studied statistics as part of my degree, and when I saw a statistic I just saw a number, not the face or the experience of the person behind the statistic. The reality for someone experiencing a mental health problem is monumental.

They will feel that mental health problem emotionally through:

- feeling out of control
- a lack of motivation
- anger and frustration
- a lack of confidence
- a lack of self-esteem
- irritability
- mood swings
- extra sensitivity to criticism
- defensiveness
- tearfulness.

They will experience it behaviourally through:

- social withdrawal
- relationship problems
- insomnia or tiredness
- recklessness
- aggressiveness
- nervousness
- increased lying
- prone to accidents

- forgetfulness
- increased reliance on alcohol, smoking, caffeine or drugs
- workaholic
- poor time management
- poor standards of work.

They will experience it physically through:

- aches and pains
- head-to-toe muscle tension
- grinding teeth
- frequent colds and infections
- hyperventilating
- feeling of a lump in the throat
- frequent pins and needles
- dizziness
- palpitations
- panic attacks and nausea
- physical tiredness
- menstrual changes
- loss of libido/sexual problems.

And they will also experience it psychologically with:

- an inability to concentrate or make simple decisions
- excessive worrying
- negative thinking
- depression and anxiety

- memory lapses
- becoming vague in their interactions and communications
- becoming easily distracted
- being less intuitive and creative.

Is this how we want anyone to feel, let alone a quarter of our population to be thinking or behaving? Your mother, father, sister, brother, aunty, uncle, friend, neighbour, colleague, you and me – that is who these statistics represent. For every number, it's a person experiencing turmoil, one way or another, as they try to navigate through life.

When I stopped seeing the number and started to see the person, I knew I wanted to do something to help and so I wanted to look at that one in four statistic as something different – I wanted to flip it on its head. So, I focused on it from a different angle:

1. What would help someone who is part of the one of four become part of the 'other three' again? – because I believe that is possible.

2. What would help someone who is part of the 'other three' prevent themselves from becoming part of the one in four? – because I believe that is possible too.

I looked at all of these signs and symptoms and knew I had to find a formula to tackle them all. I had to find a formula that was simple and could be used as a standalone process or as part of a more formal, clinical programme. I created 8Wise so you and all the other people on both sides of that statistic could take back control of their mental health, and with 8Wise Steps to a healthier and happier mind I truly believe that this can happen.

My name is Kim Rutherford, I was once part of the 'one in four' statistic, suffering with anxiety, depression and agoraphobia, and today I write this as one of the 'other three', living a happier and healthier life, the 8Wise way.

Notes for Practitioners

I knew I could never be a 'purist' therapist following only one school of therapeutic thought, which is why I chose to train as an integrative psychotherapist instead. I always held the strong belief that therapy has to work through all phases of life, the past, present and future, and I wanted an approach that could do exactly that without offending any of the great psychologists, psychiatrists and abundance of specialist therapists that help to positively change lives every day.

But even when I became qualified as a psychotherapist, I still struggled with the approach, and through discussion with my own professional supervisor, I realised I had faced similar frustrations and doubt before, but in the world of coaching. I qualified as a professional corporate coach many years before training as a psychotherapist and enjoyed the world of personal and professional development using the coaching model and I still do. From time to time, I crave a training room, and those of you reading this who have been a facilitator will understand why – the unique buzz that comes from that learning environment is hard to turn your back on forever. But in coaching the focus is primarily on moving forward towards specific goals and never really provides the support to identify and work through the root cause and current blockers.

On the flip side I found that the therapeutic model only really focused on the present or the past and there was no clear, strong focus on the future that I felt worked effectively with my clients (I appreciate you may have had a different experience). After working this through with my supervisor, I identified that a therapeutic coaching approach was the most effective approach for me to use as a practitioner, as it allowed me to merge psychotherapy principles with coaching principles for a more end-to-end holistic process that supported the client to:

- Acknowledge and accept the past and the effect it has had on their present

- Work through their current obstacles and blockers to make life feel less overwhelming and increase feelings of confidence and calmness with regards to not always feeling in confident and in control

- Develop an effective action plan with realistic goals that move them positively into the future with a set of tools and techniques to help them manage the challenges that life will bring, and help them to maintain an optimum state of mental health.

8Wise is a model that can be used for all three stages of the above process because it maps effectively to both a therapeutic model and a coaching model. Below, I have outlined how 8Wise can be used if you are a therapist supporting someone with their mental health and if you are a life coach supporting someone with managing a major life transition.

Therapists:

Below are some of the recommended processes for treating depression. I have outlined the element(s) of the 8Wise model that can be used to support with each one of the recommendations to demonstrate how 8Wise can support as a core part of your therapeutic tools, techniques and services.

1. It is recommended that clients learn about their depression. This includes understanding if their underlying symptoms are medical or not, as well as the severity of it. Using 8Wise to cultivate their intellectual wellness to do this specific learning puts the client in control of understanding their own diagnosis and being part of identifying the most effective treatment process for them too, as well as boosting an important element in their wellness spectrum, which will help with building confidence and self-esteem.

2. Any effective therapeutic process requires the client to have a social support system outside of the therapy room, as a strong social system can be an added layer of protection against depression for the client. A strong social network can reduce isolation, which is a key risk factor for depression. 8Wise can be used to develop their social wellness through cultivating strong social connections and provide the confidence to talk to trusted family members, friends, or seek out new connections. Developing effective social wellness can help the client to understand that asking for help is not a sign

of weakness and it isn't a burden to others, as well as set healthy boundaries for all future relationships.

3. Treatment for depression can take time and commitment and making that commitment feel less daunting and overwhelming by splitting it into eight focus areas can make it easier for the client to stay motivated and focussed on the process, which is what 8Wise does.

4. Lifestyle changes are an essential part of the therapeutic process for clients with depression, as it can lift the depression quicker and can be used alongside any other form of treatment. 8Wise is a perfect way to manage lifestyle change slowly but consistently, tackling each wellness element one by one and adapting and changing their lifestyle at a realistic pace for the individual.

5. By focussing on the physical wellness element of 8Wise, a client can implement regular exercise into their routine, which can boost chemicals such as serotonin and endorphins and other feel-good brain chemicals, as well as trigger brain cell growth in the same way antidepressants do. Also, a physical wellness focus with plans around nutrition and a balanced diet can keep energy levels up and minimise any mood swings.

6. Sleep is crucial as it has a strong impact on mood and brain function, which can heighten the symptoms of a client's depression such as irritability, moodiness, sadness, and fatigue. Through the physical and emotional wellness elements of 8Wise, clients can implement effective sleep diaries and learn to implement an effective sleep routine which will have a positive impact on their mental health.

Although this is not something we cover in the book, it something that is available via my website.

7. 8Wise supports the clients to identify where the stress in their lives is coming from and what possible root cause may be triggering their stress-related responses. Too much stress exacerbates depression in the present and also puts the client at risk of future depressive episodes too. Through using all eight elements of the 8Wise model to review the stressful areas in their life such as work (occupational wellness), finances (financial wellness), living arrangements (environmental wellness) and relationship issues (social wellness) you can support them to minimise the impact of those situations or simply problem-solve them effectively for their mental health.

8. As we know, some forms of psychotherapy teach the client practical techniques on how to reframe any negative thinking and inner dialogue and use behavioural skills when combatting any depression. These are the problem-solving tools 8Wise recommends clients develop as part of their mental wellness toolbelt. 8Wise focusses on using these problem-solving tools to identify and work through the root cause of the depression, helping the client to fully understand why they feel the way they do and what their core triggers are for depression. This then helps both you and the client to identify effective ways to improve emotional and spiritual wellness to stay mentally healthy.

Overall, as a therapist, using the 8Wise approach can support you and your client to identify more positive ways to handle life's challenges and problems, improving their wellness and wellbeing and protecting their longer-term mental and physical health.

Life Coaches:

It doesn't matter what type of life coach you are – you could be a relationship and family coach, a career coach, a finance coach, a mental health coach, a health and wellness coach or even a spiritual coach, because the 8Wise model can be used within the process for each of them. It also does not matter what coaching model you use, whether it be the GROW model, the Coactive model, the NLP model, the Positive psychology model or even the Ontological coaching model; 8Wise can map against all of them to help you and your client meet the desired outcome. At the heart of all coaching lies the same fundamental principles that lies at the heart of 8Wise:

- Supporting and guiding the focus of the client, towards who they are at their core, their values and their goals

- Giving them a deeper meaning to what they say, think and how they behave so they can develop more effective strategies for navigating life and initiating positive life transitions

- Helping the client to take a realistic course of action and find solutions to overcome any blockers and obstacles that stand in the way of them achieving those goals.

8Wise does this by breaking each 'life problem' into eight manageable areas and working through each of them so the end goal is holistically achieved.

For example, if a client was seeking support navigating a divorce, you could use the 8Wise model as follows:

Emotional wellness: Developing tools and techniques to manage any stress and emotions that come as a response to the process, in order to maintain positive mental health and cognitive clarity, as well as build confidence and reduce negative thoughts and inner dialogue about themselves.

Physical wellness: Implementing a healthy regime that supports in boosting mental and physical health as both will boost brain health which is needed when a divorce process can be so draining.

Spiritual wellness: Digging deeper into who the person is now after the breakdown of the relationship and what they want from their life moving forward. Understanding core values can also provide more understanding with regards to the breakdown of a relationship too, removing feelings of failure and potential confusion.

Intellectual wellness: A new life requires new learning. This starts with needing to understand the process they are in, then understanding how to separate lives and learn to do things as an individual again as well as new things that enhance them as a person through hobbies and interests.

Environmental wellness: With the breakdown of a relationship tends to come issues relating to environment. This could mean having to move to a new area, into a new home or simply having to change a once shared home into a new own home. A safe space is a crucial component when someone is going through such a dramatic life transition and that's what a focus on environmental wellness brings.

Social wellness: Break ups bring a dramatic change on a social scale, not just as the two immediate people separate but also it can affect shared friendships, wider family relationships and starting new relationships. It can feel very isolating when going through a breakup or a divorce so a focus on keeping social connections strong is crucial.

Occupational wellness: Work stress will still exist and could be heightened through the process of a divorce and so honest communication with colleagues is crucial, as is ensuring the job still meets the new goals a client sets for their new life.

Financial wellness: With the breakdown of a relationship comes a multitude of new financial burdens. It can be costly to go through a legal separation process – there may be costs involved for new living arrangements, etc., and the day-to-day living can increase when two incomes become one income. Therefore, during the coaching process, it is important for the client to manage their finances effectively to prevent the risk of financial worries causing mental health issues.

These are just two examples of the life transitions or mental health issues that 8Wise can be used for. I have also used it with anxiety, careers, starting new relationships, ending toxic friendships, relocations, merging families, starting a business, bereavement, 'empty nesters' and health issues, to name but a few.

Overall, 8Wise was developed by a practitioner to be used in practice with any presenting issue that generates high levels of stress and puts the client at risk of developing longer-term mental health and physical health issues. It can be used by both therapists and life coaches or those who are like me, therapeutic coaches who combine the principles of both therapy models and coaching models together for an end-to-end holistic approach. 8Wise can support you all. So, if you would like to implement 8Wise into your therapeutic or coaching approach then get in touch at www.daltonwise.co.uk and become part of the 8Wise family of professional practitioners.

Q & A with Kim

The common theme in all I do is the word 'wise', and I get asked about it a lot, so I thought I would answer a few of the questions here for you.

Why did you call your business Dalton Wise?

I always answer with, *'It's a family business, my husband brought the Dalton (his surname) and I bring the Wise (my wisdom).'* Trust me when I say this, it is with a big fat tongue firmly in cheek – I really don't take myself that seriously, and my husband is also very wise too, in his own way. But there is an element of truth in the answer.

What makes you Wise?

I always answer with a quote I once read which I feel sums up the journey I took: *'Yesterday I was clever, so I wanted to change the world. Today I am wise, and I want to change myself.'* I was once inquisitive child who turned into an opinionated young adult who thought she knew it all and was going to change the world. What I learnt through my own personal rollercoaster with mental health and wellbeing is that to truly change the world, you need to start changing your own world first, and from understanding this I developed a firm belief that we all have the ability to become truly wise.

Why did you call your model 8Wise?

8Wise has eight focus areas aligned with the eight dimensions of wellness, but it also incorporates philosophical and scientific discussion with therapeutic and coaching approaches which I have learnt through my professional experiences. This combination helps you make positive life changes. Through those positive life changes, you develop the power to improve your wellness and protect your mental and physical health. With this improved wellness and wellbeing comes your own path to wisdom and your own journey towards a happier, healthier and more fulfilling life, in whatever form you choose that to be.

Where is your private practice based?

My practice is based in the business district of Liverpool, England. Home of the Beatles, Liverpool FC, and some of the best architecture in the world. But, I provide online support too. Therefore no matter where you are in the world you access services from Dalton Wise.

What services does Dalton Wise offer?

Dalton Wise is a one stop shop for all mental health needs. It provides psychotherapy, hypnotherapy, life coaching, mental health and wellness training, corporate consultancy as well as the 8Wise Mental Wellness Programme. Since starting the business I have supported individuals and businesses in the UK, Saudi Arabia, UAE, Italy, Spain, USA, and Germany.

Where can I follow you?

Dalton Wise and 8Wise can be found on all social media platforms but you can also listen to my monthly radio show *8Wise Ways* on Wellbeing radio or catch me as a guest speaker on a range of international conferences. If you want to keep up to date with all the 8Wise news, tools, tips and techniques you can also subscribe to my newsletter, just head to *daltonwise.com* for more information.

Can I use 8Wise with my own clients?

My next book is for practitioners, a guide on how to use the 8Wise approach with clients. A training course will also be available to develop knowledge, tools and skills further to become an accredited 8Wise mental wellness practitioner.

Can 8Wise change lives?

Like with any change, you have to commit to the process to achieve the goals you set for yourself. But myself and many others have done exactly that and have experienced not just change but better mental health as an outcome of that. I whole heartedly believe that you can too.

Testimonials

I am not the only one living the 8Wise Way – here are just a few words from some of the amazing people who have used 8Wise to make some positive changes to their life. Some started working with me whilst in the depths of their mental health journey and others started with me from a life coaching perspective, wanting to make changes to their lives and achieve some goals. They either accessed 8Wise through the group programme or through one-to-one Therapeutic Coaching, face-to-face or online.

1. I would highly recommend working with Kim in any capacity possible. I undertook 8Wise coaching sessions during the lockdown period and her guidance, support and advice was one of the main reasons I got through it unscathed! Kim's approach made me feel instantly comfortable and relaxed. Her 8Wise approach really helped me explore all parts of my life, it helped me realise the work I needed to do on the different areas. I am well on my way after my sessions, motivated, focused and feeling closer to healing some old wounds I'd buried deep. Thank you Kim, forever grateful!

2. Embarking on a new career in a new sector could be a daunting prospect. However, Kim's support and 8Wise guidance helped me to thrive in my new role and managing an extremely stressful transition tackling any obstacles head-on. Through Kim's 8Wise coaching, I began to think more strategically, both about my own career and my life as a whole. I was able to map my personal development towards achieving career objectives and my life milestones. As a result, I felt (for the first time) that I had full ownership of my goals and my wellness and wellbeing.

3. As a manager I was struggling a lot with work stress; the support I received from Kim through her 8Wise model was entirely holistic, which was a breath of fresh air within my corporate setting. Although there was a focus on personal development, Kim was always open to coaching me through more personal aspects of my professional and personal life with the 8Wise model. I felt wholly confident in discussing any issues with Kim, safe in the knowledge that I was firmly in control of the process and the path I chose to take. I would recommend Kim and her 8Wise approach for any career, business or personal blockers you may experience. I believe that her support and the 8Wise guidance played a pivotal role in enabling me to change my life and improve my health.

4. Kim has helped and supported me to become the confident person I am today. She was my mentor and coach for two years at a time when I was stressed and filled with anxiety due to the difficulty of transitioning from university student to corporate trainee manager. Using the 8Wise approach, I found I was able to resolve my issues in an effective way. It helped me to identify who I am as a person and the strengths I have developed through my own life which I have since been able to use to improve areas of my life. I would definitely recommend Kim and the 8Wise programme as a way of managing and overcoming stressful situations in life.

5. I contacted Kim for 8Wise coaching regarding my mental health, career, personal life and how to move forward positively. I can highly recommend the 8Wise programme; Kim truly understands where I was coming from and offered really good guidance and thought-provoking questions. I have never questioned Kim's ability to empathise and fully understanding my career, aspirations or personal issues regarding family. Her experiences have helped her understand where the client is coming from. I gained a huge amount from my 8Wise sessions and thoroughly enjoyed them as Kim is personable, with good uplifting humour and spirit – she just gets it!

6. The 8Wise programmes can be summed up in one world – amazing! I left each session feeling so positive about my personal future but also as a business owner I left with a renewed self-confidence and self-belief in my own ideas and ability to manage and grow my business effectively. I feel there is structure and guidance in what Kim is providing with 8Wise for all elements, and I am ready to go! Thank you, Kim, for your help so far and I look forward to a long working relationship and support for the future.

7. The 8Wise programmes did not give me the answers, but rather, it gave me the tools to figure out the answers for myself, something which has had a significant impact on my confidence and ability to make progress within my personal life and my career. Being one of a group of ten people on the first 8Wise programme, I was inspired by how the programme could adapt to each of us depending on our mental health issues, individual work-styles and personalities. Overall, 8Wise and Kim's mentoring has made a significant difference in my personal development and I would not be where I am today if it wasn't for her – thanks, Kim!

8. Kim is a great counsellor, coach and mentor all in one, so it's not surprising that the 8Wise programme changes lives; it certainly did mine. It helped me at a difficult time in my life and I discovered that I was suffering with anxiety attacks alongside my depression and suicidal thoughts, which I hadn't realised. Using the programme, I worked through various limiting beliefs and unhelpful behaviours of mine which have been transformed so that I now show up as my best self for myself, not just other people. Now I'm creating a life and business that I love, and it's given me the stability I have longed for, all thanks to 8Wise.

9. Wow, knowledge and experience of Kim is second to none. I got so much out of one initial session that I jumped straight onto the 8Wise programme and I never looked back. It's a first-class programme that helped me to end a very toxic relationship without the overwhelming guilt I had experienced in the past, and feel like my happy self again.

10. 8Wise is a really great programme which provided me with a lot of new ways of thinking about my wellbeing and mental health. I love the 8Wise model.

About the Author

Who better to be your 8Wise™ guide than its creator, Kim Rutherford, Co-founder of Dalton Wise Ltd, a mental health and wellness support service. Mental health has been a part of Kim's life since her childhood, it's what inspired her to become a psychotherapist and mental wellness coach, trainer and corporate consultant.

She is based in Liverpool, England where she uses 8Wise™ to help her clients take back control of their mental wellness and protect their longer term mental health.

Lightning Source UK Ltd.
Milton Keynes UK
UKHW020652251022
411061UK00015B/965